# Finding God Within

## Contemplative Prayer For Prisoners

# Finding God Within

# Contemplative Prayer For Prisoners

### Raymond Leonardini

The Prison Contemplative Fellowship
is made up of prisoners committed
to the practice of Centering Prayer meditation,
as a vital form of self-transformation.

The Fellowship chose the boat as its logo,
after John 6:16-21, where the disciples are petrified,
and ask Jesus to get into the boat to save them.
He doesn't, but the boat gets them to the other side,
and so it symbolizes contemplative meditation.
Amid the darkness, and the panic, it takes us to "the other side."

For additional copies please write to:

Prison Contemplative Fellowship
P.O. BOX 6183
Folsom, CA 95763-6183
rleonardini@sbcglobal.net

ISBN-13: 978-1480266520
ISBN-10: 1480266523

*We are all prisoners*
*in one form or another,*
*and some of us are behind bars.*

## Acknowledgments

This book is a distillation of the work of contemporary masters of the Christian contemplative tradition. These great teachers of our time, whose writings are implicit in the book, include Thomas Keating, Richard Rohr, Thomas Merton, Cynthia Bourgeault, Gregory Mayers, William Johnson, Karl Rahner, William Dych, and Gerald May. Some of these spiritual masters have generously and personally brought their spirituality directly to the incarcerated. My sincere gratitude goes to them for teaching me the treasures to be discovered with persons in prison.

Thanks as well to those members of the Prison Contemplative Fellowship who in our prayer meetings over the last four years were willing to share their point of view regarding contemplative prayer in prison. Their insights form the substance of the book. In particular, I am grateful for the comments and suggestions of Harold Lawley, Lawrence Hamilton, Steven Bell, Daniel Delgado, Aaron Montgomery, William Hays, Luis Suastegui, Harvey Jacobs, G. Rodriquez, Jeff Clay, Aaron Jones, Michael Fairfax, Paul Dietering, Brad Ware, Lyle Shellman, Paul Jones, Darrell Allums, Shorty Cavanaugh, Gilbert Serrano, Michael Regacho, Eleno Castaneda, Shawn Cavette, John Honore, Calvin Mixon, Danny Van Hoosen, and Phil Darghty.

I am also grateful to my friends and colleagues who listened to my thoughts, shared their own experience, edited the material, and encouraged this work. They include Scott Wood, Chuck McIntyre, Tim O'Connell, Ellie Shea, Fred O'Connor, Jim Zazzera, Jerre Sears, Susan Turpin, Janice Boyd, Ned Dolejsi, Kathy Moore, Richard Spohn, and fellow volunteers Al Franklin, Mike Kelley, Frank Brown and Barbara Rodriquez.

Franky Carrillo, now a free man who spent 20 years in prison for a crime he did not commit, is responsible for the drawings in this book. Franky's great contribution to our classes on contemplative prayer lead to the method of teaching abstract notions of prayer through drawings.

This work could not go to press without the patience and practical insight, as well as the computer skills, of Kristi Daggett. Thank you.

Finally, my deepest appreciation and gratitude goes to my wife, Cherla, who was ever open to the ideas of the book, often made helpful editorial suggestions, and offered me encouragement to press on when I wondered if it was worth the effort.

Ray Leonardini
November, 2012

## *Be still and know that I am God*

*Psalm 46:10*

# Table of Contents

## Introduction:
## Contemplative Prayer:
## A Path to Personal Transformation

9

> *"I feel the Spirit of God moving me to be aware of feelings of hurt, joy, sadness, pleasure. I want to get deeper because the deeper I go, the more I have the opportunity to change..."*
>
> H. L.

Initials are used for statements by prisoners.
Their full name is omitted to protect their privacy.

# Introduction

## Contemplative Prayer:
## A Path to Personal Transformation

Most people understand "prayer" to be asking God for various favors -- health, safety, forgiveness, wisdom. We learn to talk to God at an early age. For many of us the only real question as we grow older is: why doesn't God answer my prayers? So frequently many of us simply stop praying and hope for the best.

Contemplative prayer is an entirely different approach to prayer. This type of prayer is based in God speaking to us, and all the techniques of this prayer focus on learning to listen to God's original language -- silence! This type of prayer is sometimes called "meditation" and is the type of prayer practiced in monasteries around the world. It is the deepest form of Christian prayer.

Listening to God turns out to be an extremely rewarding personal adventure. By trying to hold still we come to find out that God wants to communicate all sorts of things to us that we otherwise would not know. At the core, God wants to develop friendship with us, the friendship of a wise and loving Mentor, a trusted friend who always counsels us toward the right path. This is an entirely new relationship with God for most people. This relationship can be both deeply rewarding and personally challenging.

As the relationship deepens, we begin to unearth parts of ourselves otherwise unknown and avoided -- particularly those parts of ourselves we would prefer not to know -- our deeper fears, resentments, anger, jealousy, and the like. We also see more clearly our happiness and joy. As a result, through the techniques and effects of this type of prayer, God becomes a Divine therapist who knows us intimately, loves us unconditionally, and offers us a better way to live.

We find that Contemplative Prayer can work well as an 11th step in AA. This prayer practice gets to the heart of the Big Book's invitation to "Let go and Let God" by nurturing our ability to live in the present moment and just for today.

Prisoners who practice Contemplative Prayer can attest to the deep personal changes that come upon them. They find themselves at peace at deep levels, less angry, more capable of avoiding violent responses, more willing to find positive alternatives to frustrating circumstances, and able to address life-long patterns of resentments and grief.

Contemplative Prayer does not assume a particular religious faith, nor a particular prayer or Bible background. The only requirement is a willingness to explore the inner path to a relationship with God.

*Nothing in all creation is so like God as Silence.*

### Definition of terms.
The terms meditation, contemplation, Contemplative Prayer, and Centering Prayer are used interchangeably throughout this book. They are all words that describe a unique, deeply Christian form of prayer. While there are differing root meanings for each word, they give way to a general sense of this prayer as a wordless waiting in silence for the Presence of God as we understand God.

**Part One** of this book deals with the notion of Contemplative Prayer itself: what it is, how do we do it, what can we expect if we practice Contemplative Prayer, and wheather it makes any difference in our life.

**Part Two** is about living a daily contemplative life, and the practical effects of a contemplative life style. This part addresses the realities of prison life from a contemplative vantage point. It explores the spiritual journey that emerges from our prayer practice. It deals with a new awareness we develop as a result of our prayer practice. Personal experiences, up to this point hidden from us, can come into our awareness in a way previously unknown to us. Sometimes, it can appear that we are going backward in our spiritual journey. The reality is wholly different. In fact we discover that recalling the personal traumas that emerge are in fact a sign of progress. If we know the medicine will first make us sick, then restore us to our original sense of health, we are less likely to stop taking the medicine. Part Two affords a road map for the journey.

**Part Three** suggests a contemplative view of the Gospels. It reflects an entirely different way to approach the understanding of Scripture and the spiritual life. It helps us gain a new perspective on what our journey means to us. As a contemplative practice takes hold for us we find that Gospel truths are much more about changing our view of the way God works in the world than about commandments and laws of behavior. We see Jesus in a whole new light. The faith of Jesus in the Father becomes our model to see how God works in the world.

Reading Scripture as a prisoner with a Contemplative Prayer practice brings discoveries and insights consistent with the deep knowledge of God gained in contemplation. As we find the God Within in Scripture, we come to see that our morality and integrity follows almost naturally from God loving us first.

The plant is on a perch in a high corner of
Greystone Chapel in Folsom Prison.

*The Elephant Ear* by Franky Carrillo

"This vibrant and beautiful plant is still able to grow, flourish, and
bring happiness to those who take the time to gaze on it in such a
dark place. This growth is occurring in a mere handful of soil, held
in a tiny space--the pot--the cell--prison. I found the symbol of the
plant rang true in my life. It gave me a sense of God's presence.
The stick is in the center of the pot, the center of someone's life,
where one can lean on, find support, and give it a firm foundation."

Franky Carrillo

14

# Part One

## Contemplative Prayer and the Inner Journey

### Who am I?

If we take a good look around us, we see that we are each a totally unique person in this world. Because we are in prison, we may have several external characteristics that look the same, but deep down inside no two of us are alike. Scientists now know that our brains also form a unique pattern -- no two brains, with billions of electrical impulses, are the same. No other person has the same experiences, or the same reactions to our experiences. Our inner life is deeply our own, difficult to know, and hard to talk about.

This is especially true with the dark and negative parts of ourselves. This area is often off-limits for talk in prison. Most of us go our way trying our best to avoid any such reflection. We march on down the line keeping any suggestion of personal change at arm's length. We let our addictions and phony self cover over and shout down the whisper of a new view of life.

Yet for some of us we find that in Contemplative Prayer God attends to our very uniqueness and communicates a certain friendship to us. We find a new confidence in our self. What comes up for us as we sit in silence appears to be exactly the exchange God desires for us, and the exchange we want as well, although we don't yet know the language of Silence.

In our quiet moments we can see the arc of our life. We see the trajectory of our choices. We may even be able to grasp the reality that we often do what we don't want to do, and don't do what we truly want to do. Yet we seem to be able to cut ourselves some slack.

Many of us have found deep relief, even tolerance, for this desperate part of ourselves. We found this relief, not by giving up our usual religious and spiritual practices. Rather we found relief by the simple practice of resting in God. We sit without words, without promises, without shame, without even fully knowing what is happening to us, except that we have turned toward God, the Ultimate Mystery in our life. We've learned to be still.

> *God carries each person along a different road, so that you will scarcely find two people following the same route in even half of their journey.*
> John of the Cross, *The Living Flame of Love,* 3:59.

## How Do I Stop Talking and 'Listen' to the Silence?

Wise spiritual masters through the centuries, people who are no different than ourselves, offer simple methods to come into Silence. Even before the modern discoveries of psychology and the science of how our brains work, these wise teachers found that holding still in Silence is a natural part of discovering who we are.

We have all been told, at one time or another in our life: "Just be yourself," even though exactly how to "be yourself" was never clear. The same suggestion applies to listening to the Silence in Contemplative Prayer. We are invited to do nothing, even though doing nothing is an entirely foreign notion for us. This is especially true when it comes to a relationship with God.

From our earliest years we are taught that God is watching us. We are told to do certain things, think certain things, and pray certain things to have a relationship with God. It was all up to us. Contemplative Prayer offers an entirely different approach: by doing nothing, by sitting in Silence, we allow God to take over and fashion our lives as was originally intended. We begin to see God as a loving father, rather than and angry judge, or abusive parent.

It is as if our inner selves naturally needs a frequent vacation from the on-going inner chatter. We have come to recognize that Silence is an essential part of our being. We don't have to do anything! The remarkable power of Contemplative Prayer descends on us as we do nothing. We simply have to get out of the way to allow our inner self to find the space it is craving.

> *"It's like being in the eye of a storm. For that time (during Centering Prayer) it is being quiet in the presence of God. It allows me to quiet down when I'm flooded with words."*
>
> A.M.

# Centering Prayer: A Simple Path to Contemplation

Centering Prayer is a  simple method with easy to follow steps. This simple method leads us gently into resting in God, the essence of Contemplative Prayer.

For some of us, right at the start, we found it hard to believe that it could be so easy. We believed our 'monkey' mind could not be denied. Yet, we too came to see that Centering Prayer is not about the absence of thoughts. It is, rather, about the distancing or detaching from our thoughts. (The term "thoughts", by the way, refers to memories, feelings, imaginations, insights, to-do lists, our private script about our life -- all the chatter and emotions that come into our mind.)

Detaching from thoughts is like watching TV in our cells. When someone comes to talk, our focus changes (detaches) from the TV. We don't listen to the TV, may not be aware that it's even on. So it is with whatever thoughts or feelings that arise during Centering Prayer. We learn not to pay attention to them.

For others of us, before we tried Centering Prayer we are vaguely worried that this type of prayer will change our personality. We worry that somehow we'd be different in a strange way. Perhaps we thought we'd become more reclusive, less spontaneous, more pious. On other levels, some of us worried that by developing an open, listening relationship with God that God would ask something of us we simply could not give.

We learned that none of this is true. In fact we found the opposite: the practice of Centering Prayer put us in touch with our truest self, the self underneath so much of our false values and notions we carry around with us. We found, at the same time,  a God inside who braces us on our journey. We learned that we are not so bad at the core after all, maybe there is goodness in us that comes naturally. Centering Prayer gave us back to ourselves.

# In Silence: How Do I Do That?

In Centering Prayer our goal is to let go of all thoughts and just be in Silence, deep within us -- not only not saying anything, but not intentionally thinking about anything. When we close our eyes to meditate, it is natural for all kinds of thoughts and feelings to fill our minds. We expect this, we let them come and let them go.

HERE IS THE SECRET TO BE ABLE TO DO THIS: before we begin doing the prayer, we choose a word, a simple word of one or two syllables. This becomes our "sacred word," not in a religious way, nor like a mantra used as a concentration technique, but sacred in its meaning to us. Words like peace, love, joy, trust, and listen. Some prefer breath, life, yes, mercy, or any word that helps us to let go of our thoughts. Then when thoughts begin to come we just repeat our sacred word silently a few times and let the thoughts go by.

This word is the only word we use in meditation. By distancing us from our thoughts, feelings, and emotions, it serves as the symbol of our willingness, our consent, to move into our truest self, the self that opens to Presence deep within.

> *"The use of the sacred word really hooked me in. It allows me to focus on one thing and let all other thoughts and feelings go. It's as if there is Someone else inside of me that wants me to do only His agenda."*
> S.B.

> *"As you know we are back on lockdown ... I sat for about an hour this morning when my mind was all over the place. By the end, I wasn't upset and I really was at peace ... It was as if God was leading me to see how much I was letting the craziness of this place disrupt my peace of mind..."*
> H.L.

# What Am I "Consenting" To?

Consent is the heart and soul of Centering Prayer. Our use of the sacred word is a short-cut, an almost mechanical reminder, that our intention is to hold still in Silence. We know that this holding still allows God's presence and action to take over.

In other words, we detach from our usual internal dialogue, with all its judgments, story-lines, hidden hurts and prejudices, and let God's Silence do the talking. Using our sacred word we simply and gently move into an entirely different space in our on-going relationship with God.

We soon see that our sacred word represents our deepest intention to be open to the divine life within us. This intention of ours is more valuable than the craziness of our attention. This willingness to be quiet with Presence allows the Divine life already within to move us deeper.

With stillness comes acceptance. Acceptance brings a letting-go at our core. Personal change begins in earnest.

> *The desire to consent to God's presence within us, does not come from our initiative, but from the grace of God. We do not have to go anywhere to find God because He is already drawing us in every conceivable way into union with Himself. It is rather a question of consenting to an action that is already going on in us. To consent to God's presence is His presence.*
>
> Thomas Keating, *Open Mind, Open Heart*, p.36.

# How to Do Centering Prayer

1.       Set aside a time for your practice, 20 minutes is the goal but do what is feasible, twice a day if possible. One time is better than none. (It helps to have a timer to avoid having to wonder how much time has passed.) Times prior to count or chow work well.

2.       Sit comfortably on a chair, bunk, or on the floor with your back against the wall, or even facing the wall.

3.       Close your eyes and begin to settle down into that deepest center of your being. Take a few deep, slow breaths to help you relax and stay loose. Silently introduce the sacred word as the symbol of your intention to consent and surrender to the Presence within you.

4.       As thoughts and feelings rush in, silently and gently repeat your sacred word until they go by.

Thoughts are normal, don't try to stop them. But when they come use your sacred word to release them. At the beginning of your practice you may use your sacred word often. This gets easier with time.

If you find yourself sleeping or drifting into sleep, bring your attention back with your sacred word. At times your sacred word will simply drop away.

# Neither Resist Nor Retain Any Thoughts

After a period of time, we learned that we cannot stop thoughts, or other feelings, from coming up during meditation. They simply arise on their own. Any forced attempt through will power ("I'm not going to think or feel that...") simply doesn't work. We learned not to be surprised by any manner of thoughts or intense feelings coming during Centering Prayer. We don't resist them.

Because they can carry us away from our Silence, we use the sacred word to release them. Our deep selves know that retaining these thoughts or feelings just takes us out of our Silence, and leaves us with the same old story of our lives.

As we learn Centering Prayer we come upon a truly remarkable discovery: this practical prayer method, detaching from our thoughts, is the key to our own freedom in our daily life. It is like a duck raised as a chicken. The duck never knew swimming came naturally until he found himself in water! The simple act of doing nothing and being nothing (no thing) as we sit in God's Presence frees us to be the unique person we were created to be.

> *Centering Prayer is the cornerstone of contemplative commitment. This prayer creates the space of openness and receptivity where God actively participates by living our life for us, and we become a conduit for Divine Energy to move into the world.*
>
> Thomas Keating, *Centering Prayer.*

## What Happens During Centering Prayer?

As in any relationship, the more time spent with the other person, the more we come to know them. Our experience is no different with the God of our understanding, only it is harder to talk about it. Because we enter into Silence there are no words to describe the experience. We can become aware of God's presence and action in our lives. But talking about it can be extremely difficult.

For some the experience is like a vast empty space of tranquility and safety. For other people the experience is like a cloud descending on them. This description is not new. One of the first books ever written on this type of prayer was written by an anonymous author in the 14th century called The Cloud of Unknowing. Notice it is called the Cloud of Unknowing, not not-knowing. We learn plenty about ourselves, particularly our hidden, repressed selves. Our 'knowing' is in the gut, not the head.

As we sit in Centering Prayer, distancing ourselves from our words and thoughts, we find that immediate evaluations of our prayer practice is not helpful. It is like asking fish to describe their experience of water! As a result, we don't judge our periods of Centering Prayer as 'good' or 'bad' by the times we use our sacred word, or the amount of distractions we encounter. Similarly we recognize that our experience of Presence is not depending on feeling God's presence.

> *"The best part of Centering Prayer for me is to just sit and say my sacred word. I know I could ask God for anything, but I just sit and know that God loves and cares for me."*
> G.S.

" When I do Centering Prayer I can spend time in eternity so that the small things in the temporary world are not so hard to deal with. When all the "boats" (my thoughts) go by, carrying all my feelings and pain, and I don't get on the boat, I'm on the eternity side. But the greatest thing for me with this practice is that now I'm not afraid to approach God."

L.H.

As a method of meditation, Centering Prayer is founded upon the gesture of surrender, or letting go. The theological basis for this prayer lies in the principle of kenosis (Philippians 2:6), Jesus' self-emptying love that forms the core of his own self-understanding and life practice. During the prayer time itself, surrender is practiced through the letting go of thoughts as they arise. Unlike other forms of meditation, neither focused awareness nor a steady witnessing presence is required. There is no need to 'follow' the thoughts as they arise; merely to let them go promptly as soon as you realize you're engaged in thinking (a "Sacred Word" is typically used to facilitate this prompt release).

Cynthia Bourgeault,
*Centering Prayer and Inner Awakening*, p. 162.

24

# Engaging the Silence:
## Going Back to Go Forward to Freedom

As Centering Prayer becomes a regular practice, as we "rest in God" free of pre-conceived words or notions of what we need from God, gradually our rigid defenses begin to change. Our usual thought-patterns and ways we experience consciousness start to shift. At first we are surprised to see the shift and wonder: "when did I start thinking this?" Or, "I haven't thought about that painful event in years!"

These thoughts and images arise as much outside Centering Prayer time, in our daily life, as during our prayer time. Since we detach ourselves during prayer time, and feel no urgency to process the narrative during that time, we find the experience comes up during our daily routines. Our prayer practice has loosened deeply embedded experiences.

For those who are not familiar with these effects of Centering Prayer, it can feel like we are going backward into events and story-lines we thought we had overcome. Here we are, for example, feeling lost in grief or anger, when we thought we had all this under control. If not recognized as progress, this can be severely discouraging: "why do I always feel like I've screwed up?"

Patience helps us see this discouragement comes from our bogus view of what it means to be a man. Society would have us believe we should avoid all our painful experiences at any cost. Yet in meditation we learn we are freeing ourselves from our constant story-line streaming in our mind, and we are actually learning something new about our self.

We discover that some of the routines in our life -- the music, TV, games, and so forth, serve as a way of avoiding these very experiences. Feeling and seeing them now is actually a good thing. The space we create in Centering Prayer, as we detach from thinking, now is the space we need to encounter our deeper selves -- the material lodged in our unconsciousness. We have new-found personal freedom. We know ourselves in a way not known before.

While remembering and re-living past memories may seem strange at first, we come to see that this is the direct route to personal healing and change -- the type of transformation we always vaguely knew we needed, we just didn't have the means to get there. We come face to face with our false self.

> *"Centering Prayer allows me to deal with all those events and memories that I have chosen to avoid, especially the painful and shameful ones. I find as I deal with them, little by little, they lose their power over me."*
>
> D.D.

# Our Human Condition: The False Self

As the human family has developed and evolved over time, we are learning that much of our personal experience, particularly the deeply painful events of our childhood, is buried deep within our own personal unconscious, separate from our conscious awareness, and seemingly inaccessible to our rational will-power.

This personal unconscious contains all the self-serving habits that have been woven into our personality from the time we were conceived; all the emotional damage that has come from our early environment and upbringing; all the harm that other people have done to us knowingly or unknowingly at an age when we could not defend ourselves.

Also in this deep, secret part of ourselves, are the methods, the programs for happiness, we acquired at an early age to protect and defend ourselves to ward off the pain of unbearable situations. It makes sense that we develop these methods as infants because our survival is at stake. The strategies are all about our basic needs for survival, esteem, affection, power, and control. Because they started as infants, we think that these plans are actually part of our "self." Unfortunately, these unconscious programs that we needed to survive when we were defenseless, don't hold up in a world of 7 billion other people competing for the same things. That's why these happiness plans are called "false."

The early false self methods grow into sources of motivation for happiness. They are made much more complex as we grow into adulthood, and reinforced by our social environment, our parents, neighborhood, schools, churches, and the like.

The heart of the struggle with our false self-- that part of ourselves that does what we don't want, and doesn't do what we do want-- addresses our unconscious motivations for happiness. If we do not recognize these hidden influences, the false self will simply adjust to our "new" way of life, and nothing really changes. Even if we commit to Christ, we still pursue our need for security, success, and power only this time in a Christian context. The false self unconsciously follows us into whatever lifestyle we choose.

The good news is this: we can find happiness, and relief from our false self, by looking in different places. As we become more aware of these false programs, we begin to see our unhappiness is in our false plans, not in our self, or how others treat us.

---

*"My first experiences with Centering Prayer were boring. But over time I realized that it began to give me more control over how I responded to all of life's situations. It allows me to see why living in the chaos of our addictive thinking never achieves any enlightenment at all. The best part of the practice is the self-control and insights I have found. I have patience and forgiveness for the 'failings' of others."*

H.J.

---

## What is this False Self and Where Did It Come From?

The false self describes the self we make to cope with the emotional experiences of early childhood. We came into our world with instinctual needs to stay alive. Our instincts tell us, even before we can think, that we need food and tenderness from our mother. Our basic instincts teach us to cry when we need help -- all this from the moment we are born.

As we grow our basic instincts grow more complex. Our physical and emotional needs become more complicated as we begin to think on our own. These needs develop in the context of family and neighborhood which has their own particular view and idea for meeting these basic human needs. When these needs aren't satisfied when we are young, without our realizing it, we make our own programs to satisfy these needs. Some call this false self the "homemade" self -- it is the best we can do with our inner experience. We do it because we believe that our very survival is at stake, and in some inner sense, our survival is at stake.

This "homemade" false self is subtly influenced by early childhood trauma. These traumas are common for all of us. It has little to do with the intentions of the adults around us. All we know as a child is that our mother may not come to us when we cry, or that we should be afraid of our father. We may be exposed to, or directly experience, abusive events so painful we unwittingly dump them immediately into our unconscious. These early childhood traumas, combined with our unmet instinctual childhood needs, supply the energy and driving force of our adult attempts at happiness.

What happens next makes a lot of sense: we invent a self necessary to address these losses. If we did not get the affection we craved as a child, we'll look for it everywhere as an adult: we look for a wife who will treat us like she is our mother. Or, we'll be the best athlete at any cost to get the recognition we never felt from our father. Through Centering Prayer we come to see that these attempts at happiness won't meet the need that created them.

29

*"Centering Prayer has taught me how to resist feelings of anger that come from officers and inmates. In my time of silence I have learned to dump my trash and let God fill my life with his peace. Our trash can be very hurting and confusing if we don't understand it is the false self talking and not your comforting God."*

H.L.

# Centering Prayer Unravels the "Homemade" False Self

As our Centering Prayer becomes a frequent practice for us, the motives of our false self become noticeable. In our daily life, we begin to find our homemade selves everywhere! The impenetrable concrete wall separating our conscious thinking from our unconscious buried material, developed over a lifetime, begins to soften by our Centering Prayer practice. The power of our false self that originates in our unconscious becomes observable. Those memories, too painful to remember, hidden in our unconscious, begin to slowly emerge.

This happens more in our daily life than during prayer. All of a sudden we remember long-forgotten events buried in our memories. This time they appear with a certain perspective that has "space" around it similar to the "space" we create around the thoughts and feelings that arise during Centering Prayer. It has that particular quality in our gut that attracts us to the event in ways we have never experienced before. We feel less afraid.

While the event may still hold the sting of the long-ago repression, we somehow find the courage to let it come into our full consciousness. We learn to let it teach us what it wants to teach us. We don't really know what that is, but somehow our willingness to stay with it allows us to be present to it in a way we have never be able to do. Much of our inner experience is beyond words and concepts so that we have a hard time finding words to describe this, even to ourselves. Yet we know deep movement is happening within.

Usually for the first time we grasp how entirely self-centered our plans actually are. We learn that we have placed ourselves at the center of the universe, as if the world exists to meet our needs, and have asked God to kindly go along with our plans. Of course, this is exactly opposite to reality, and opposite to the true way that happiness can come to us. We learn from hard-won experience that we have it upside-down and inside-out. True happiness comes to us, not in a self-centered world, but in a world that has our experience of the Divine plan in the center.

> *"The power of Centering Prayer has granted me courage to face the demonic forces of lies that deceived me from childhood until today. It gives me the confidence to confront and discern the lies that I face within and from without on a daily basis."*
>
> A.M.

> *"The fruits of this practice are obvious when you compare the attitudes of those who practice Centering Prayer with those of the general prison population... I think God speaks to us subtly in our lives. If we aren't listening we might miss it or even doubt his existence. Centering Prayer is a stubborn child who patiently sits before the Father not to be ignored, waiting to feel His love."*
>
> P.D.

## The Release of Pain: The Way to Live the Divine Plan

The letting-go part of Centering Prayer steps forward to help us change our self-centered view of life. Although we maintain our separation from thoughts and feelings as we do Centering Prayer, the benefits are most available in our daily life. Now we are able to enter a room deep inside, even though it had been locked up tight, bolted, and nailed shut. The door swings open! Now the denials and avoidances in our life begin to naturally surface on their own. As we walk the yard we remember an act of kindness to us we hadn't thought about in years. We begin to grasp patterns of behavior throughout our life that has caused us pain, anger, and grief. We see the sunset in a fashion we'd never seen before.

As our psychological material of a lifetime rises to the surface, we witness a new sense of self emerging on its own that neutralizes the pain. From somewhere deep inside we begin to say: "maybe I'm more OK than I ever thought." "Maybe God does love me, the real me."

As we rest deeper in God in contemplation, ever so subtly our self-image begins to change and shift. Feelings, memories, painful recollections -- all the hidden material of a lifetime -- start to naturally discharge into our awareness. Sometimes as a gentle stream, at other times a tidal wave. The vast storeroom of our traumatized self is opening to Divine therapy: a gentle encounter that allows us to patiently mull over the experience of a life-time.

We recognize a subtle principle at work in our contemplative practice: there is an unmistakable connection between experiencing traumatic events in our past and a sense of our own deep, at-the-core, goodness. "Made in the image of God" takes on new meaning for us in our gut as well as our mind. We discover we actually do have the humility and courage for the personal change we crave. We find we experience hope at deep levels, hope that allows us to continue our spiritual journey in earnest.

# Our True Self: God's Tattoo

When we first become familiar with notions of the false self, and the havoc we see it create in our life, we can't get rid of it fast enough. Our first thought is to find the road leading away from all the complications resulting from the decisions produced by our false self.

But as we progress in our prayer practice, we discover something different. Our "true self" is already with us. It lies buried underneath the programs and projects created by our desperate search for happiness.

We don't have to empty the bottle, so to say, before we can fill it. We learn that our truest self is a natural, God-given, orientation waiting to be tapped and released from our inner self. As we watch our futile attempts to hang onto our plans for security, esteem, and control, we more readily see how useless they are. We see our fierce grip on anger begin to loosen. We observe our own activities with a new-found objectivity that allows us to see our part in relationship struggles. "Maybe I actually did have something to do with this conflict...!"

When we get caught again in the activities and motives of our false self, as we frequently do, we return to our prayer practice for re-orientation. We find compassion coming out of us without even thinking. We begin to see ourselves in the people around us, even including the guards. ("Looks like he is having a bad day...") We find that we can cut people some slack that we previously never dreamed of.

The space developed in Centering Prayer gives us a freedom rarely experienced before. Our ability to let go of conflicting emotions during prayer allows us to let go of them in our daily life. This spaciousness brings us, without effort, into a greater awareness of the enormity of the present moment. The goals and outcomes of our plans seem less important. We find now that we can actually live in the "present moment" in a fashion not known before.

Now we understand the old adage:

The past is over,
the future is not here,
I have only the present.

Our experience tells us that the present moment holds everything for us. The true self emerges from within ourselves. It doesn't come suddenly, like turning on a light switch. It is a gradual birth of a part of ourselves long buried. This part of us is the DNA of God in our life. This is what is meant by the "image" of God. It is the spot where God has forever tattooed us with God's own specially recognized sign that we belong to God. Now when we are undecided about a course of action in our life, holding still in the present moment unlocks enormous potentials. The butterfly is emerging from the cocoon. Nothing will be the same again.

> *"I don't have the opportunity to talk to other inmates in the SHU, so Centering Prayer and the Contemplative Fellowship is really important to me. My spirit is free .... and I am always with you during your Monday night meetings."*
>
> L. S.

> *"The Centering Prayer class lets me take time to focus on my spiritual journey. I love this class because it teaches us to stop trying to please our false self and begin to feel fulfilled. I feel closer to my Spiritual Destination then ever in my 32 year old life."*
>
> G.R.

*The biblical basis for*
*Centering Prayer is Matthew 6:6*

*"When you pray*
*(when you're looking for*
*the right relationship with God),*
*go to your inner room*
*(the deep center of yourself),*
*and pray to your Father in secret*
*(without words),*
*and your Father who sees in secret*
*(is with you at your core),*
*will reward you*
*(grant you your heart's longing).*

# Part Two

## Living a Contemplative Life

Our weekly gathering for Centering Prayer and discussions on the contemplative journey is essential to our prayer practice. In the meeting we listen to each other and learn that no two of us have exactly the same spiritual journey. We look the same, dress the same, go through the same daily routines, yet we see and hear in our meetings that the Divine works with us in personally distinctive ways.

For some of us we are immediately thrust into an awareness of the pain in which we live. Once we turn off our head-phones and TVs, and try to go inside ourselves free of distractions, we are surrounded and immersed in the very pain we have tried to avoid. Our pain seems to emerge from a life-time of disappointments and poor decisions, like a drain that is backing-up. We have a whole new awareness of the addictions that have driven so much of our decisions.

For others of us the awareness is like stepping into the sunshine after years of darkness and cold. We find joy and satisfaction in the smallest of things. Seeing a friend on the yard, a casual letter from home, the memory of someone long-forgotten -- these seem to bring us a deeper sense of peace than previously known.

We recognize in our meetings that our life now is a mixture of joy and pain. We learn that no experience, no matter what, has the power to completely and finally take away the access we have developed into our inmost self. Once afflicted, we have only to reach into our prayer practice for the contact with our self and the spaciousness now awaiting us there. We find that our practice of Contemplative Prayer is portable. We take it with us wherever we go; our cell, the SHU, the yard, wherever.

As individual as our journey is, we find out that we are a lot alike. That is why we call our group Prison Contemplative Fellowship. The companionship we experience together, free of economic, educational, and racial boundaries is like few associations we have in prison.

*"I look forward to the group circle and the different ethnic backgrounds of the group. We all understand that we are in a safe environment. The safety and security of the group still remains the same after all these years.*

*My practice of Centering Prayer gives me a deep awareness of the 'balance' of God's creation – gifts of warmth and cold, the seasons, the colors. Even in the darkness and loneliness of prison Centering can take me to good places."*

W.H.

# The God Within

The goal of Contemplative Prayer of "waiting on God," or the promise of "resting in God" through a practice of Centering Prayer, seems strange and awkward at first. What is this "waiting" or "resting"? Isn't our relationship with God mainly about "doing" and "acting" in a way consistent with God's commandments?

Actually, resting in God (Contemplative Prayer) invites us to a wholly different relationship with this Ultimate Mystery we call God and Jesus called Father.

For most of our early life our view of God is unconscious and unexamined. The God of our youth, taught to us as children in hundreds of subtle ways, and for many reasons, through our Churches, teachers, parents, and our own fantasies, looks very much like any other authority figure! If we've had problems with authority figures we tend to imagine similar problems with God. Our thoughts of God may be positive, even loving, but in the back of our minds we know this God has the upper hand, absolute power and control of everything, and always watching us.

Scripture describes another view, and contemplative prayer gives us a method. Jesus' most frequent commandment to His followers when speaking about God is: do not be afraid! For Jesus, it is not about reacting in fear to this powerful God, but opening to the Divine Presence already deep inside waiting for us.

This is the view of the Father described in the Lost Son (see a summery of Luke15:11-32 on the next page), the starting point for a contemplative prayer practice. In fact, this view (the God within) is the deepest driving force in Jesus. His stories consistently challenged His listeners to throw off the God-to-be-afraid-of and accept a different view of God. We need to listen and do the same.

Instead of trying to impress and earn the respect of this controlling God, it is about looking inside and accepting the invitations from the God that loves us, as Fr. Greg Boyle says, "no matter what." Instead of looking at our material goods and thanking this God for blessing and rewarding us, we look within at our relationship with this loving God and realize the blessings of the "poor in spirit," and the "meek and merciful" (Matt. 5:3-12).

This actual awareness of God as Father is the promise of Contemplative Prayer, and the value of the practice of Centering Prayer.

*In the Parable of the Lost Son (Luke 15:11) Jesus tells the story of two sons. The younger one runs away from his father, does everything he can to ruin himself, and is completely "lost". The other son does everything right, at least it seems that way. When the "lost" son recognized the enormity of his mistake he decides to go home and be a servant to his father. While still "a long way" away, the father, who night and day was hoping exactly for this return, catches sight of his son, runs to him and embraces him even before the son can ask for forgiveness. He says we'll have a party in your honor because you've come home.*

*The other son is not so excited. He figures he is not appreciated because he has done everything right and no party is thrown for him. His father tries to explain to him that his son was "lost" and is now home. That is all that matters.*

## The Challenge of Centering Prayer

The practical obstacles to doing Centering Prayer are many and obvious. Starting any new practice demands, at the very least, a decision to change our comfortable routines and familiar ways of living life.

Somewhere in the back of our minds the practice of Centering Prayer can bring a vague fear of silence and what may lie beyond and within this silence. Sometimes doing Centering Prayer just seems boring! When we enter our traditional way of praying, at least we know what we're praying for, at least we know what we are putting before the God we believe in. But with Centering Prayer we can sometime get a hazy thought that God may ask something of us we are not willing to do. Or, that we will have no experience whatever of God.

The fear, actually, makes a lot of sense because in Centering Prayer we are going into our own wilderness, and, on some level, allowing ourselves to experience our personal loneliness, broken relationships, and failures. If we make a habit of hiding these realities from others, and from ourselves, of course any change in our pattern will create a sense of anxiety and fear.

In the beginning, our curiosity will help us overcome these initials fears and anxieties of a new relationship with God. As we progress, and experience God at deeper levels, courage and determination will keep us going.

Prisoners do overcome these initial fears and start a Centering Prayer practice. We start for various reasons: some because we want to change the direction of our spiritual life, others want to try something besides words. We experience a kind of curiosity about this different type of prayer where words are less important and "listening" is emphasized.

As we develop a meditation practice our routine consciousness expands to now include seeming irresolvable conflicts in our relationships. We seem to experience conflicts with a new awareness. For example, we think: "how can I continue to have an active relationship with my daughter when her mother doesn't want her to have contact with me?" Now, instead of going off on how poisonous her mother is relative to us, we can truly appreciate her point of view. We seem to gain a "space" around the conflict that contains more appreciation for the complexity, with greater patience for finding an outcome consistent with the complexity. This "space" (what some masters call the Spaciousness of the Divine) contains alternatives and strategies we had not yet anticipated.

We discover in our difficulties with Centering Prayer, as with other self-development tools, hidden and unrealistic expectations can do us in. These expectations grow like lawn weeds -- hard to see at first, but if left to grow unrecognized, can take over the patch. If we can view these expectations directly, we can treat them as any other thought during Centering Prayer. Treating these excessive expectations in this fashion reduces their energy and lessens their control over us.

> *"Every time I try to meditate I hear all the noise around me, I get angry, and I can't get myself still to even say my sacred word"*
>
> W.M.

> *"After nearly 40 years of incarceration I certainly did not believe I possessed the ability to meditate. The thought of relinquishing trust to someone produced anxiety, insecurity, and disbelief. But today I'm good to a point. I still harbor many trust issues, but through my meditation practice I'm working continuously to overcome these emotions."*
>
> S.C.

# The Seeds of Peace

The practice of meditation (centering prayer) is an invitation to deep, personal freedom. The obstacles in developing a meditation practice are the very same obstacles in developing our sense of personal freedom. We are drawn to meditation as we are drawn to any practice (spiritual, physical, emotional) that promises to give us relief from that deep, nagging, negative self -- the continuing experience of being less than who we truly are and who we want to be.

Yet, we are surprised when our first experiences in meditation bring up parts of ourselves we are trying to forget: our anger, fear, jealousy, sense of competition, and pride. These emotions are usually embedded in the stories that come as we sit to meditate. We begin with our sacred word and immediately we are annoyed at the level of noise around us, or we remember how disappointed we are that someone did not pay sufficient attention to us, or disrespected us. Then we find ourselves back years previous when a teacher humiliated us, or a parent yelled and shamed us for reasons we do not recall. Now we feel worse than before we began to meditate. Some of us ask: why would I want to meditate only to have these painful experiences emerge in my mind? Aren't I trying to not remember these things? Isn't "not remembering" what peace is all about?

Inmates who have overcome these beginning obstacles to a meditation practice tell us that there is a critical added ingredient as we sit and endure these painful memories: we feel some vague sense that we are more than that person in the story. We are not only that humiliated and shamed child; there is something more to us that all our negative, mental narratives suggest. What can this ingredient be? As we gently return to the sacred word, we let these painful memories arise and fade away, aware they may come again. We trust that there are other, deeper parts of ourselves that gives us courage to face our shame and fear. Slowly and gradually this trust emerges as an experience. Maybe the Divine does actually love us after all! Maybe I'm a lot more than that humiliated child.

These are the seeds of peace. This is the draw of meditation that invites us to a profound freedom that is totally our own, not based on opinions or judgments from others. These "seeds" come from our deepest Self and are the lasting gift of a meditation practice.

"Through the practice of Centering Prayer a miraculous transformation takes place that I have not experienced in any other spiritual practice. In my opinion, it seems that this transformation can only happen through contact with God's divine grace and love. Centering Prayer is a conduit to God's love and caring nature. Given time, the manifestation of these principles is tangible."

M.F.

"It's all about 'the Circle' for me during lockdown. I see The Boat picture and it reminds me of the circle we sit in when we meditate on Monday nights. It gives me strength to continue to open myself to God's presence."

B. H.

*The Prison Contemplative Fellowship is made up of prisoners committed to the practice of Centering Prayer meditation, as a vital form of self-transformation. The Fellowship meets weekly to pray and share the events of their spiritual journey.*

*The Fellowship chose the boat as its logo, after John 6:16-21, where the disciples are petrified and ask Jesus to get into the boat to save them. He doesn't, but the boat gets them to the other side, and so it symbolizes contemplative meditation. Amid the darkness, and the panic, it takes us to "the other side."*

Meditating alone in our cell can seem like an inner, self-centered act that has no impact whatsoever on anyone else. In fact much of the language that teaches meditation and contemplative prayer focuses on our uniqueness and the individual ways the Divine Healer works in our life. This is one of the extraordinary parts of Contemplative Prayer. We need rely on no one for our meditation practice. Lockdowns, in some respects, make it even easier to do our meditation. We have fewer choices to distract us.

There is another view: a contemplative practice brings outside, other-centered movement. This Divine Healer works with us individually for sure. Yet there is no doubt that God entrusts us to each other in similarly healing ways. We hear helpful remarks from someone in the group; they give us helpful suggestions on how to deal with various parts of a meditation practice; or, they talk about their own inner journey in a way that opens for us a deeper appreciation of our own journey. We find ourselves sitting in amazement at the wisdom coming from another prisoner.

At other times, someone can be unaware of the ways they inspire us. A simple act of kindness can have a profound impact on our awareness, and create in us a desire to go deeper into our practice. We become present to each other in the Silence. We come to understand that our impact on each other is not coincidental. It is the way the Divine Healer works in our life. How could it be otherwise?

> *"Praying in a group has had more meaning for me, than doing it alone. I am amazed at the transformation that occurs, and the depth of spiritual wisdom and commitment. Meditation with the Fellowship is exciting and unbelievably sincere."*
>
> F. B.

# We Are Not Our Thoughts

*All methods that lead to contempla-tion are more or less aimed at bypassing the thinking process. The reason is that our thinking process tends to reinforce our addic-tive process - our frenzy to "get something" from the outer world to fuel our compulsions or to mask our pain. If we can just rest on a regular basis for 20 to 30 minutes without thinking, we begin to see that we are not our thoughts. We have thoughts, but we are not our thoughts. Most people suffer because they think that they are their thoughts and if their thoughts are upsetting, distressing, or evil, they are stuck with them. If they just stopped thinking for a while every day as a discipline, they would begin to see that they do not have to be dominated by their thoughts.*

Thomas Keating, *Intimacy with God*

The simple technique of movement away from thoughts and feelings during meditation by use of the sacred word demonstrates for us a revolutionary notion: we are not our thoughts. We find many of our self-inflicted, false-self dominated conflicts are the product of a never-ending, mental commentary on the people and events around us.

When we experience the separation between our selves and our "thoughts," we tend to let ourselves off the hook of negative self judgments. We begin ever-so-subtly to realize that we are not as bad off as we sometimes feel, or as some people tell us we are.

We also begin to notice a space between our thoughts and our choices for action. In fact, sometimes we can see that no matter the thought, even a thought that triggers some deep emotion in us, we don't have to do anything. Something valuable happens inside of us when we don't do anything! This notion is really foreign to much of the so-called wisdom of the day that says we must be "forceful men of action" or "decisive" or "leaders."

This discipline of not identifying with our thoughts is the foundation of the new awareness we find in ourselves outside of meditation. Its as if we find new breathing room for the multiple thoughts and emotions we carry with us all the time.

The quiet and deep movements inside of us, usually kept in the background, now have room to express themselves. The "space" that we discovered in Centering Prayer, now provides the meeting place for us to deal with ourselves in a new and creative way. "When did I start thinking about that?" "How is it I'm not inclined to do this anymore?" "This 'personal' conflict is really not about me."

The simple exercise of releasing thoughts as they arise in Centering Prayer has an enormous pay-off in our life. It is the key to a personal freedom that cannot be taken away, or prohibited, or locked-down.

# Meditation Impacts Returning to Prison

It is well known in the criminal justice literature that the practice of meditation is a critical factor in whether a prisoner will return to prison after release. The research seems to indicate that this fact is true no matter the type of meditation practice. Why?

Centering Prayer meditation practice says it like this: sitting in silence for 20 minutes twice a day, a person begins to experience in daily life two important discoveries. The first is that God actually does love and care for us. This is not a realization like turning on a light switch. It is an experience that comes less noticeably, but often it comes quickly. It may come in a chow line or on the yard. Early on, the meditator begins to realize we actually do have our own specific and unique relationship with God, and God does seem to be taking an interest in us.

The second discovery is connected to the first. The meditator begins to understand and appreciate the poor decisions we have made in our life. This discovery arises free of guilt and shame, in a way that the meditator can actually begin to see our life with new eyes. It's like a reviewing our life in a relaxed conversation with a friend whose opinion we really trust. We know that our friend has always had our best interests at heart. We can listen without retaliating.

Centering Prayer calls this experience the "unloading of the unconscious" because it is an un-loading (a natural emergence) of materials we've held within ourselves for a life-time. It is really an un-burdening of our deepest secrets in a way that allows them to emerge into the light of day. When it does reach the surface it comes into the setting of acceptance and compassion as with a relaxed conversation with a friend. We can actually view our personal experience without drowning in self-hatred and self-contempt.

When we experience this un-loading during Centering Prayer and return to our sacred word, we experience the actual freeing of ourselves from a life-time of torment and self loathing. Somehow we are saying to ourselves that "yes, this may be true, but it is not the whole story, there is much more to me than this..."

From this point of view, personal problems are easier to see and resolve. Behavior that is arising out of deep personal turmoil is seen for what it is. We are now more likely to treat ourselves with respect and compassion. We have the habit of going into our spaciousness where personal choices are unlimited, and returning to prison is a poor choice among a host of positive choices.

---

*"Meditation is a call to salvation and resurrection for me. Without it I'm in the desert fighting for my life, under attack from within..."*
A.M.

---

*"I came to Centering Prayer class for help and insight in dealing with feelings about life. I guess I needed to be OK with being not OK.*

*For me the practice of contemplative prayer means a never-ending journey. There is always some new break-through. Everything that is not you and not God disappears into what is God or God's love. When I come out of meditation I feel like I bring more of God's love back with me."*
L.H.

# Behind the Masks We Wear

In classical times actors wore masks on stage. The audience could readily see, by the mask, the emotion (and maybe even the intentions) of the actors. The Greek word for this mask is the origin of our word "person." Notice it isn't the real inside emotion or intention of the actor, only the mask. By birth and training we are all "actors" in this sense. We wear various masks for various situations. Over time we begin to believe that the mask we wear is actually who we are! We think it is our authentic self.

As we start a spiritual practice like Centering Prayer, we begin to see the person behind the mask. In the beginning this can be upsetting, even terrifying. Is there this much falseness in me? Is there anything of me beyond the mask? We launch more seriously now into the realm of the false self in action.

Actually it is not only the false self that we see. It is really greater self knowledge we are gaining, not just the uselessness of the false masks we wear. Our new-found ability to see the excessive strivings for security/survival, affection/esteem, and control/power, means we have developed a deeper degree of self awareness. As some men put it: our consciousness is expanding.

We see the mask because, at the same time, somewhere inside we know our "trueness." We need not be discouraged by the size and depth of our false self, or the many subtle ways the false self is injected into our intentions and actions. Something "true" is emerging at a deeper level.

Once we become aware of the masks we wear, the simple sitting in stillness of a practice like Centering Prayer gives us the needed strength of heart, the courage, to move through our experience of falseness. We somehow find a way, or a 'way' is given to us, to move on and through our experience of falseness.

Though we rarely experience it at the time, in truth as we reflect back on our change in awareness, we begin to see the work of the Divine healer and the remarkable emergence of our true self. The transformation of the self now begins in earnest.

> *"The same emotions that trap us in our unhappiness are guides to the transcendent. It all depends on how we view them -- as resistance to change in our personal status quo or as invitations to surrender our ego control. These emotions are hints that there is something immeasurably more to life than what I've yet discovered or experienced."*
> Gregory Mayers, *Listen to the Desert: Secrets of Spiritual Maturity,* p.39.

# Our Own Private Oasis

Listening to prisoners with a Centering Prayer practice we seem to agree that our meditation creates some sort of quiet oasis in the midst of the noise and intensity of living in prison. We are able to go to this oasis despite the really loud clamor and the blare of TV and music. For many of us, this quiet place is the goal of meditation. We find respite here free of the madness surrounding us in prison.

This oasis is an ever-expanding inner space that is the place where we meet our truest self. This space has a depth and breadth that increases as we develop the habit of meditation. Several experiences emerge in this vast inner space.

The first is the awareness that events of our day, particularly the events of conflict, are not meant to be taken personally. We get a sense that whatever is confronting us is not really about us! It may be about whatever is bothering the person we meet. We somehow "know" (in this inner space) that it is not about us, even when it seems to be directed specifically to us. And, further, we don't know how we got to this point of view, but we believe it anyway!

The second experience in this inner space is a growing tolerance of the poor choices we have made in our own life. We have a new point of view that recognizes how really misinformed we have been. We "see" ourselves with much greater clarity, and see how we bought into attitudes and patterns of behavior that hurt us and hurt others. We begin to see the action of the "false self" in our life.

We learn that the spaciousness we have inside ourselves is also a place of remarkable creativity and peace. We come to trust this place as a spot of decision-making for those really complicated problems we find in our daily life. Rather than immediately reacting to the events that trouble us, we find new resources for coping when we enter this space. For some of us it feels like our own 'control room' where we find choices we might have missed otherwise.

We can enter this space free of any solutions to our predicament, with an attitude of patient waiting, and find alternatives that seem to fit our deeper self. Over time this oasis becomes a daily destination. Our prayer periods increasingly feel like a necessity for good health. If we miss a session, we recognize the loss of a chance for deep inner rest. We don't feel an obligation to do centering prayer, it has become integral in our daily life for a feeling of wellbeing and clarity.

> *"When I started the practice of Centering Prayer I noticed I wasn't nervous. I saw that nothing was expected of me. I could figure this out at my own pace. All I had to do was be open-minded, and see that there is no wrong way to connect myself with the Divine... I can do it anytime, day or night, working or exercising. It brings me back to me."*
>
> C.N.

## The Divine Therapy

We all want a vacation from ourselves. We want to get beyond the chatter, the noise, the constant inner commentary we tell ourselves. For most of us the commentary is negative, that is, our reactions to the mini events in our lives seem to remind us that we are not good enough, or did things the wrong way, or screwed up again in some fashion. That's one of the reasons why we watch TV, put on headphones, and try to lose ourselves in any number of distractions. We want to get away from ourselves.

This is not a new experience for us. We see that this need to get far away is the origin of many poor choices and bad decisions. As we sit in our cells we can feel the poison of discouragement slowly invade the vital organs of our life. It invades our Centering Prayer practice as well: why am I doing this? I'm not getting anything out of this. I'm still angry...

Yet still on some days when we sit in our prayer group circle we hear the whisper of hope. What do we have to lose? Where else can we go, really, to turn around the down-ward cycle of our life?

We find new appreciation for Contemplative Prayer as a prayer without words because our pain and discouragement is greater than any imagined advice or instruction. As we hold still we begin our own private therapy session with the One we are waiting for, the one who knows us through and through. These meetings at our inner core are the medicine for the poison that is debilitating our spirit.

We know that Centering Prayer is not the simple, easy road to bliss. It takes courage to face the pains and struggles of a lifetime. When we enter this personal space, all the false notions of ourselves are there to welcome us! All the false promises of our addictive behavior and our phony thinking are waiting for us. We come to understand that we can only change the way we see things by dealing directly with our pain and confusion. We find that facing this pain in Centering Prayer removes some of its sting.

After a time, we notice that an almost imperceptible change enters our life. We are less fearful of the pain. We see that by not resisting the pain, nor holding onto it, it starts to fade. Moments of relief emerge. We find that we can grasp the part we play in our own down-ward spiral. These "therapy sessions" empower our recovery. The transformation we crave is at hand.

> *"The best thing about the practice of Centering Prayer is my time alone with God."*
>
> A.J.

> *Religion is largely populated by people afraid of hell; spirituality begins to make sense to those who have been through hell, who have drunk deeply of life's difficulties.*
>
> Richard Rohr, *Things Hidden,* p.100.

*Africa: Osun Procssion* by Betty La Duke

*Lord, you search me and you know me, you know when I sit and*
*stand, you understand my thoughts from afar.*
*My journey and my rest you mark. You know all my ways.*
*Even before a word in on my tongue, Lord, you know it all.*
*You formed my inmost being, you knit me in my mother's womb,*
*my very self you knew!*

Psalm 139

> *The Gospel truths invite a degree of trust in God that seems impossible in the so-called real world. And they require the most awful and awesome spiritual sacrifice: letting-go of control.*
>
> Gerald May, *The Propaganda of Willfulness*

# Part Three

## A Contemplative View of the Gospels

For the first 12 to 13 centuries after the life of Christ and the writing of the Gospels, his followers would gather together to hear the Word of God. This was not simply because most people could not read. They heard the Word together because they found a method of hearing the Gospels that brought the text to life.

One would read a certain text, pause in silence, then slowly read the text again. The listeners would hear a phrase repeated again and again. It would sink into their memory and imagination. ("I am the good shepherd.") In the context of prayer and openness to the Word they would sit and let the text marinate through them.

They would sit in silence and let the text take them to the place they needed to go. Because they were familiar with silence, and Contemplation was a familiar form of prayer, they could "rest in God" as the text worked them. Since they were engaging their memory and imagination they would by-pass a strict rational analysis of the text. For these listeners, the text had more than one meaning. How the text opened them was the goal.

Through this practice called Lectio Divina (Sacred Reading) the Gospels invite us to a degree of trust in God that seems impossible in today's so-called real world. As this process flows in us we find that gospel truths are much more about *metanoia* (a Greek word the Gospel writers used that means changing our view of the way God works in the world) than about commandments and laws of behavior. These gospel truths lead us to the great spiritual sacrifice: letting go of control and putting our lives into the hands of God.

The following gospel passages prompt us to take another view of the wisdom sayings of Jesus. We begin to notice more clearly Jesus' own contemplative practice of "resting in God" when he prayed. His prayer relationship well summarizes the source of his wisdom and ours as well.

# The Contemplative Jesus: Model for Meditation

It took the early Church nearly 300 years to define and write an acceptable explanation of the divine and human Jesus. Their formula leaves a lot out, as it simply states: Jesus was fully human and fully divine. His divinity was the same as the divinity of the Father. His humanity was like ours except he was without sin. His divinity did not substitute for his humanity, and his humanity did not take the place of his divinity. Rather, Jesus modeled for us how to be fully human, and as such how to become divine.

With this as background, his prayer practice takes on new light. As a human person he had to find his human identity (Who am I?), and figure out how his identity related to God (Who is God?), the way we all do, by trusting his inner experience of the divine and by study and conversation. As we read scripture for hints of this "experience of the divine" we find Jesus spent long periods of prayer "throughout the night." Although he taught his disciples the "Our Father" as the necessary way to approach the Mystery he called "Father," there can be no doubt that he would not spend those long nights in prayer simply repeating the "Our Father" over and over again – it wouldn't be human.

If he was truly "human" (like us), and encountering the demonic, healing the pain of the sorrowful, and trying to get through to his religious leaders of the day – as he did, then he must have needed that time of night to sort out his relationship with the Ultimate Mystery. Who am I? Who is God? and Who am I in relation to God? must have been the core pursuit of his life.

Is our life any different? Our core questions in figuring out the central meaning of our existence are the same? Isn't this the central theme of our contemplative practice? Could it be any different for him? Jesus found his answers in contemplation. Can it be any different for us?

We find the faith *of* Jesus is as important as faith *in* Jesus.

# A Nobody Announces a Somebody

> Mk 1:1-8
>
> The beginning of the gospel of Jesus Christ, the Son of God. ² As it is written in Isaiah the prophet:
>
> *"Behold, I send my messenger ahead of you,*
> *who will prepare your way;*
> *³ the voice of one crying in the wilderness,*
> *'make ready the way of the lord,*
> *make his paths straight."*
>
> ⁴ John the Baptist appeared in the wilderness preaching a baptism of repentance for the forgiveness of sins. ⁵ And all the country of Judea was going out to him, and all the people of Jerusalem; and they were being baptized by him in the Jordan River, confessing their sins. ⁶ John was clothed with camel's hair and wore a leather belt around his waist, and his diet was locusts and wild honey. ⁷ And he was preaching, and saying, "After me One is coming who is mightier than I, and I am not fit to stoop down and untie the thong of His sandals. ⁸ I baptized you with water; but He will baptize you with the Holy Spirit.

The writers of the four gospels had a real problem on their hands: how to start writing about Jesus and to prepare their readers for the deep realities of his life.

All four of the gospels use a dramatic character to announce the coming of Jesus. He is like an announcer who comes out before a play and prepares you for the drama that is about to unfold. Even the two gospel writers (Matthew and Luke) who start their gospels by describing Jesus' birth, and the miraculous events surrounding it, eventually get to this "announcer" when they describe the adult life of Jesus.

Who was he? John the Baptist. He was not a priest, not a religious authority, not a member of the temple. He apparently had no earthly power or position, no wealth, no powerful family background. He had no special education, was not living in the center of a dominant culture. In short, he was a nobody. An odd person for God to choose to announce the coming of His Son, our savior liberator.

Well, then, what did he have to say? Again, oddly, his words are strangely confusing for the setting. The writers tell us he came as a "witness" to "testify" on behalf of Jesus. Witness and testify are legal terms, as we well know, used in court to prove or deny one's innocence. Is Jesus already accused? Of what? What is going on here? Can this John be a credible witness if he had no power and religious authority? How do we know? Would you believe him?

Yet, without any official authority from the recognized religious leaders of the time, the temple officials, John performed the deeply religious ritual of baptism and exhorted his followers to a "repentance for the forgiveness of sins." Probably just like his listeners at the time, down through the centuries we have grossly misunderstood the core meaning of this "repentance for the forgiveness of sins."

This "repentance" is less about guilt and shame for our mistakes and bad decisions, and more the root notion of a change of heart, or a change in the way we see life and live life. John is saying start looking with different eyes; open your life to an entirely different way of living. Leave behind the many ways we dissipate and narcotize the divine energy that comes to us. Be willing to change the habits and character flaws that prevent the divine breaking into our lives. Change the way you behave; be prepared for a radically new way of relating to God and each other.

Now this is starting to make sense in light of John as the forerunner of Jesus. Knowing what is to come, and the profound words and actions of Jesus, we need a new way of looking at life to be able to comprehend the enormity of the invitation coming to us in the person of Jesus. The Jesus that John is announcing is not another "nice" religious person, irrelevant to our deepest fears and most personal conflicts. On the contrary, John is preparing us for a reality we can easily dismiss, and not even see, if we use our normal, habitual way of living life.

John is saying this is no ordinary prophet coming to Israel, like so many others who have guided them in the past. No, this is the One Himself. This is the One to bring us into the depths of relationship with the Divine, a depth so intimate and complete that with Him we can call God "Father" and God can call us "Son."

How would you announce his coming?

## The Initiation of Jesus

> **Mark 1: 7-11**
>
> [7] And he was preaching, and saying, "After me One is coming who is mightier than I, and I am not fit to stoop down and untie the thong of His sandals. [8] I baptized you with water; but He will baptize you with the Holy Spirit." [9] In those days Jesus came from Nazareth in Galilee and was baptized by John in the Jordan. [10] Immediately coming up out of the water, He saw the heavens opening, and the Spirit like a dove descending upon Him; [11] and a voice came out of the heavens: "You are My beloved Son, in You I am well-pleased."

The Gospel of Mark is an in-your-face, fast-paced narrative of the life and death of Jesus. The beginning of the story in the opening chapter describes Jesus' encounter with John the Baptist. Jesus approaches John without fanfare, presenting himself simply as one needing baptism. Remember, John the Baptist was preaching to large crowds around Jerusalem. He urged repentance and conversion. He demanded a change of heart and mind to be ready for the coming of the Holy One. John spoke as a messenger to prepare the way for Jesus of whom John said he is not worthy to fasten his sandals.

This opening story illustrates a deep confusion surrounding the identity of Jesus. Why, if Jesus is the One, would he be presenting himself to John to be baptized? Baptism then, as now, is a deep and significant initiation into a new way of thinking, leaving one's old life behind, and committing to a new way of living. If Jesus was fully human and fully divine, as we have come to believe, why did he ask for baptism?

One tradition in the Church answers the question by pointing to the words that Jesus heard after his baptism: "You are my beloved

Son; with you I am well pleased." This tradition focuses on the revelation, spoken from the heavens, that Jesus is the Son of God. This revelation invites us to follow Jesus because he is God's Son.

But another tradition looks at this story and wonders what Jesus must be experiencing to even approach John for baptism. As a fully human person, Jesus' own inner experience prompts him to reach out to John. Apparently, like the others seeking John's baptism, Jesus wants this "change of heart and mind." He is looking for a way out of his sense of separation and disconnection. He must feel a deep, inner draw to God. As a human being, He probably is feeling the need to be identified with something or someone greater than himself. For Jesus, this is the inner movement of the initiation we call baptism.

Whatever his inner motives, it is clear that his life was radically changed when he emerged from the waters of baptism. He could not go back. After hearing the words of the Father, the next story in the gospel tells us that Jesus had to go into the desert to begin to assimilate the new experience. His baptism was a major event that influenced the course of his life. He now responds in ever-deeper ways to the invitations of the Divine.

It is no different for us. The dramatic events in Jesus' life are reflected in our own life. We experience from time to time a sense of disconnection and separation from others, as if there is some "design defect" in us. We too experience an inexpressible longing for wholeness and healing, a need to go out of ourselves. At least a part of us is drawn in the same way as Jesus was drawn to baptism by John. Our invitation is one and the same as Jesus' invitation into the life of God.

Like Jesus, the experience of deep initiation begins to address our deeper longings, and profoundly changes the course of our life. Take a close look. We are not making this up. We are responding to a deep, inner need for wholeness. The holy ones tell us that God gives us the desires he intends to fulfill in us. Listen closely and hear the words spoken to Jesus, the same words now spoken to us: "you are my beloved Son; with you I am well pleased."

> "It is not preach a deep message and you will be rejected; be rejected and you will have a deep message."
> Richard Rohr, *Things Hidden*, p.101.

# A Most Threatening Proposal

Matthew 25:14-30

[14] For the kingdom of heaven is just like a man about to go on a journey, who called his own slaves and entrusted his possessions to them. [15] To one he gave five talents, to another, two, and to another, one, each according to his own ability; and he went on his journey. [16] Immediately the one who had received the five talents went and traded with them, and gained five more talents. [17] In the same manner the one who had received the two talents gained two more. [18] But he who received the one talent went away, and dug a hole in the ground and hid his master's money.

[19] Now after a long time the master of those slaves came and settled accounts with them. [20] The one who had received the five talents came up and brought five more talents, saying, "Master, you entrusted five talents to me. See, I have gained five more talents." [21] His master said to him, "Well done, good and faithful slave. You were faithful with a few things, I will put you in charge of many things; enter into the joy of your master."

[22] Also the one who had received the two talents came up and said, "Master, you entrusted two talents to me. See, I have gained two more talents." [23] His master said to him, "Well done, good and faithful slave. You were faithful with a few things, I will put you in charge of many things; enter into the joy of your master."

[24] And the one also who had received the one talent came up and said, "Master, I knew you to be a hard man, reaping where you did not sow and gathering where you scattered no seed. [25] And I

was afraid, and went away and hid your talent in the ground. See, you have what is yours." [26] But his master answered and said to him, "You wicked, lazy slave, you knew that I reap where I did not sow and gather where I scattered no seed. [27] Then you ought to have put my money in the bank, and on my arrival I would have received my money back with interest. [28] Therefore take away the talent from him, and give it to the one who has the ten talents." [29] For to everyone who has, more shall be given, and he will have an abundance; but from the one who does not have, even what he does have shall be taken away. [30] Throw out the worthless slave into the outer darkness; in that place there will be weeping and gnashing of teeth.

As a good teacher summarizes his teaching, Matthew's gospel in Chapter 25 gives us a final summary of Jesus' teaching.

Not surprisingly, Jesus uses a parable to teach clearly what he is all about. Parables emphasize and grab our attention away from the normal way we think of ourselves and our life. In Jesus' time, his parables shocked his listeners into a whole new way of thinking about deep and important life themes. These parables of Jesus had an extra teaching bonus: they showed how Jesus' own life was consistent with the radical teachings of the parable stories.

This parable of the "talents" is no less radical and shocking than the others. What appears to be an unjust punishment of one servant is an accurate description of the outcomes of fundamental choices in our life. To appreciate this outcome, realize that the word "talents" in the parable, literally meaning coins of value, really means something of great personal value. Jesus' listeners would understand that he was referring their long-held religious traditions and beliefs.

In particular, when Jesus referred to the "talents entrusted to the servants" he was describing entrusting to his disciples all his life teaching -- his total human experience -- about the Father, living in union with the Father, and living a life of selfless loving with each other. Jesus' "possessions" were nothing other than the totality of all he lived and taught before he was arrested and executed.

From this perspective it is easier to see how the two servants who did something with their masters "possessions" (v. 14) were actually then doing something with the entirety of Jesus' experiences and teachings. They of course would be rewarded for their risk-taking with double their initial gift, greater responsibilities, and their "master's joy". In other words, by taking the risk and incorporating Jesus' teaching and living as He did, they would experience themselves the depth of the joy experienced by Jesus. By giving away love and kindness they would find themselves with ever greater depths of love and kindness.

The opposite is true for the one who in fear of this master buried his initial possessions. "Buried" means he did not accept the invitation and take the risk of living his experience of Jesus. He was unable to overcome his fear of changing his habitual way of acting and thinking. He couldn't leave his routine to respond to the invitation of Christ. His one talent was taken from him, not in punishment, but because this is what naturally happens when fear controls our life. The parable wants us to observe paralysis of fear to encourage us to take the risk to push fear into the background.

"For to everyone who has, more shall be given, and he will have an abundance; but from the one who does not have, even what he does have shall be taken away." (v.29) This is the "shock" of the parable. This seeming unjust conclusion is not unjust at all. It describes perfectly the reality of following the life and teaching of the Master Himself.

# The Decontamination of the Temple

John 2:13-22

[13] The Passover of the Jews was near, and Jesus went up to Jerusalem. [14] And He found in the temple those who were selling oxen and sheep and doves, and the money changers seated at their tables. [15] And He made a scourge of cords, and drove them all out of the temple, with the sheep and the oxen; and He poured out the coins of the money changers and overturned their tables; [16] and to those who were selling the doves He said, "Take these things away; stop making My Father's house a place of business." [17] His disciples remembered that it was written, "zeal for your house will consume me." [18] The Jews then said to Him, "What sign do You show us as your authority for doing these things?" [19] Jesus answered them, "Destroy this temple, and in three days I will raise it up." [20] The Jews then said, "It took forty-six years to build this temple, and will You raise it up in three days?" [21] But He was speaking of the temple of His body. [22] So when He was raised from the dead, His disciples remembered that He said this; and they believed the Scripture and the word which Jesus had spoken.

Occasionally, Jesus' behavior is so unpredictable and apparently violent we can wonder who this person is. Such is the case with today's main reading, traditionally known as the Cleansing of the Temple. This cleansing is so deep and thorough we should describe it as a "decontamination" -- a clearing out of life-threatening, toxic materials.

It is important to note that this reading is from the fourth gospel, the gospel of John, and it is radically different from the first three gospels in its portrayal of who this person Jesus is. The Jesus of the Matthew, Mark, and Luke is the wisdom Jesus, whose insight and intimacy with the Ultimately Mystery (God) is so close that Jesus calls God his "father". With the fourth gospel, Jesus goes beyond this intimate relationship to claim the he and the father are one and the same. What can we make of this? Can we possibly believe the claims of Jesus in this gospel?

John's gospel story gives us valuable clues to understand the depth of the mystery Jesus is laying out to us.

Remember the Temple was the central place of worship for the Jewish people. An entire cult of worship had developed around their worshiping practices. It was based on the assumption that the vast majority of people were sinners, that is "unclean," and needed temple worship to be cleansed.

The religious cult obligated them to make amends through sacrifices of sheep, oxen, and, for the really poor, doves (pigeons) for their unclean status. Conveniently, the authorities made the rules, sold the animals for sacrifice, and mediated their connection with God.

This sacrificial cult, the people thought, was the only way they could come to God. At root, the religious authorities convinced the people that their relationship with God could only be mediated by the authority's permission. If the poor and excluded didn't follow the rules, they were not "justified" or in right relationship with their God. The rules were extensive and governed everything from eating to praying to worshipping. All freedom of personal intimacy with God was removed.

It is this attitude and belief in the impossibility of approaching God directly that is at the root of Jesus throwing out the merchants and bankers from the Temple. He is not simply driving out the merchants and religious authorities, he is redefining at the deepest level how we can approach the Divine. It is not some clarifying of an essentially helpful religious practice, it is a totally different perspective on how to live in union with God. This driving out of the temple authorities was nothing other than a redefining of the entire Temple ideology, the core of Jewish religious practice -- a through toxic decontamination.

Jesus' total rejection of the authority's teaching on how to enter into right relationship with God prompts them to ask: where is your authority to be doing and saying this? Jesus' "destroy this temple and in three days I will raise it up" totally confuses them even more, as they say that it took 46 years to build the temple. But it gives us a final clue to his meaning and motive.

The gospel writer is telling us, with Jesus' words, that from now on the Jerusalem Temple, which has been turned into a marketplace, has been replaced by the risen body of Jesus as the true holy place. As with the experience described of Jesus, we may encounter the Divine, first and foremost, in the depth of our own hearts, in the awareness of the Transcendent One dwelling within us.

This is good news for us. Following the risen Christ, we Christians know that we can go directly to intimacy with God in our deepest selves. We come together in the body of Christ to share in the Body of Christ. As Jesus and the Father are one, we too, through our union with Christ, become one with the Father as well.

"The purpose of contemplation is neither to improve our morals or ethics nor to perfect our personality to win friends and influence people, nor any kind of self-improvement or self-aggrandizing goal. The 'purpose' of contemplation is to lose our self: 'He who saves his life loses it, while he who loses his life for my sake discovers who he really is.' "

Gregory Mayers, *Listen to the Desert*, p.41.

## After Our Death: What can we Expect?

> ### John 6:37-40
>
> [37] All that the Father gives Me will come to Me, and the one who comes to Me I will certainly not cast out. [38] For I have come down from heaven, not to do My own will, but the will of Him who sent Me. [39] This is the will of Him who sent Me, that of all that He has given Me I lose nothing, but raise it up on the last day. [40] For this is the will of My Father, that everyone who beholds the Son and believes in Him will have eternal life, and I Myself will raise him up on the last day.

No matter the religious or cultural perspective, death, that of our loved ones' and ours is the topic we avoid most of the time. Let's not avoid it here. Let's find what meaning it has in our life.

John 6: 37-40 is one of the most complicated passages of the fourth gospel and offers a helpful perspective. Remember this fourth gospel is like no other gospel, written by someone in a community that was formed around someone who knew Jesus personally. This gospel describes a Jesus who comes talking about "eternal life," coming from the Father, and going back to the Father, and taking us with him. He seems to have a lot to say about death.

In the chapters preceding this passage, the religious authorities of the time find Jesus to be different from the religious leader they were expecting. The Jewish leaders wanted a political leader, Jesus preached non-violent love. In fact, Jesus did not seem to go along with many of their religious doctrines or rules for religious observance. So they were constantly asking for a "sign," or proof, that he was the real thing. He gave them a sign, but not the one they wanted. The more he talked, the more confused they became. Who is this person? Where did he come from? What sign does he need to give us?

They ask him for a sign comparable to the manna (bread) given to their ancestors in the desert by Moses. Jesus follows up on the request by telling them that there is in fact a "new manna" given by the Father, and that "new manna" is himself! This new manna will give life to the world. This new manna, this bread of life that gives life to the world, is God's revelation of Jesus. It is God's nourishing Word, when accepted and lived, that becomes the source of life.

So Jesus continues: "everyone who sees the Son and believes in him may have eternal life, and I shall raise him up on the last day."

Accepting the revelation of Jesus as the full embodiment of God's unconditional love for each one of us is the central core of all Christianity. It is the best "sign" we receive. By accepting this revelation, living a life of unselfish love, we are told that we will not die, just as Jesus did not die, but we will be raised up, just as Jesus was raised up, by the Father. Can I believe this? Is this passage credible with my own experience such that it gives me hope for overcoming my death and the death of my loved ones?

We must ultimately ask ourselves: Is Jesus credible? Is his message true? Could Jesus actually be the person that is God's Son? What theology and creeds tell us is one thing. Our experience of the Divine in Contemplative Prayer, just as Jesus' experience of the 'Father' in his Contemplation Prayer, gives us a whole new level of understanding of our ultimate destiny. We can, like Jesus, come to accept our experience as a promise of life without end.

## To Whom Am I Indebted?

> **Matthew 22:15-22**
> [15] Then the Pharisees went and plotted together how they might trap Him in what He said. [16] And they sent their disciples to Him, along with the Herodians, saying, "Teacher, we know that You are truthful and teach the way of God in truth, and defer to no one; for You are not partial to any. [17] Tell us then, what do You think? Is it lawful to give a poll-tax to Caesar, or not?" [18] But Jesus perceived their malice, and said, "Why are you testing Me, you hypocrites? [19] Show Me the coin used for the poll-tax." And they brought Him a denarius. [20] And He said to them, "Whose likeness and inscription is this?" [21] They said to Him, "Caesar's." Then He said to them, "Then render to Caesar the things that are Caesar's; and to God the things that are God's." [22] And hearing this, they were amazed, and leaving Him, they went away.

Jesus is heading into his final days. He is now in Jerusalem, the center of religious practice, preaching in the Temple, the holiest place for the religious people of his time. In a few days he will be arrested, convicted, and executed.

He speaks of God, the Ultimate Mystery, in a way like no other. He calls God his "Father," and tells the poor and marginalized (the "unclean") that God is their Father as well, they are full heirs and participants in the Kingdom he describes. Moreover, he criticizes the religious authorities for their hypocrisy and deceit, for using their authority in ways that misguide their followers. For this. the religious leaders want to discredit him before his followers and entrap him in a violation against the Roman authorities.

So a delegation of religious leaders set a trap. They would use the tax law and the use of Roman coins. (A Roman coin had the inscription "August, Son of God" in tribute to Augustus Caesar, the Emperor of Rome. For any good Jew, it would be idolatry to use this coin, and a sin against their God.) So they approach Jesus, and after flattering him, ask him: "Is it lawful to pay the census tax to Caesar or not?" They knew that if Jesus said 'yes' he would be considered a collaborator with the Roman authorities, and be despised by the devout religious Jews. If he said "no," he would be considered a subversive, subject to arrest by the Romans.

After holding the coin, Jesus said: repay to Caesar what belongs to Caesar, and to God what belongs to God. He side-steps the question, and raises a still more serious challenge to his questioners and to us. In effect he tells us to: repay the one to whom you are most indebted! That is, repay your obligations to the one who is most important to you, the one from whom you get your most personal self-definition. For a good Jew at the time, this could only mean God, since the very core of their religious belief was that they were God's chosen people. They were silenced by his answer.

Before we are too quick to put down the religious authorities trying to trap Jesus, we all would do well to ask ourselves the same question: where is my allegiance, to whom am I indebted? How do I define my deepest self?

Recently a prisoner whose parole date was rejected by the Governor just 48 hours before his release told me: "they have my body, but they don't have my mind or my spirit." He didn't define his deepest self as a prisoner.

How would we respond to Jesus' challenge? To whom am I most indebted? What defines my deepest self?

All things are possible with God.

---

Mark 1: 40-45

[40] And a leper came to Jesus, beseeching Him and falling on his knees before Him, and saying, "If You are willing, You can make me clean." [41] Moved with compassion, Jesus stretched out His hand and touched him, and said to him, "I am willing; be cleansed." [42] Immediately the leprosy left him and he was cleansed. [43] And He sternly warned him and immediately sent him away, [44] and He said to him, "See that you say nothing to anyone; but go, show yourself to the priest and offer for your cleansing what Moses commanded, as a testimony to them." [45] But he went out and began to proclaim it freely and to spread the news around, to such an extent that Jesus could no longer publicly enter a city, but stayed out in unpopulated areas; and they were coming to Him from everywhere.

---

During Jesus' time, anyone with a skin disease would be considered a leper, automatically declared unclean, and set apart from their community. Any contact with a leper would render a person 'unclean' as well. Lepers remained isolated and excluded from their community. Yet, with a simple human touch, Jesus heals the leper and restores him to his community.

Notice the leper came to Jesus and "begged" him for healing. This leper, alone and isolated from his family, had hit bottom, he could sink no further. Hearing about Jesus' wonderful healings he came to believe that Jesus could heal him as well. In a real sense, he had already turned his life over to Christ even before he met Him. The leper knew that Christ could heal him and remove his uncleanness. He was ready for a fundamental life shift.

Jesus did not disappoint him. He touched him! Imagine. No one touched lepers. It was forbidden by the religious authorities of the day. Yet, this compassionate touch of Jesus both healed the leprosy and restored the man to his kinfolk. He was no longer unclean.

What part of our life needs such healing? As prisoners we know the pain of segregation from our community. We can imagine our own personal encounter with Christ, just as the leper in today's Gospel. We can imagine what we would say to Him given the chance.

> *"Only one who is patient and does not drown out the frightening Silence in which God dwells can hear and appreciate something of the eternal life already given to us."*
> Karl Rahner.

# Life in the Prison Wilderness

> **Mark 1: 12-13**
> [12] Immediately the Spirit impelled Him to go out into the wilderness. [13] And He was in the wilderness forty days being tempted by Satan; and He was with the wild beasts, and the angels were ministering to Him.

Prison inmates understand what it means to live in the wilderness. It's a place that is stripped of life's routines and activities to the degree that only the raw necessities of life remain. In prison, as in the wilderness, one is subjected to powers greater than themselves. And subjected in a fashion that allows only submission to these powers greater than themselves.

Why in the world would Jesus be drawn to the desert? Remember He had just received an extraordinary initiation by John the Baptist where He heard the words: You are my beloved Son; with you I am well pleased. Why would the same Spirit draw him into the desert, a wilderness filled with danger and the threat of death?

Jesus' experience in the desert is another initiation into His mission as the Father's Son. Instead of beginning His preaching immediately after His baptism, He begins His preaching after His desert experience. He learned something in the wilderness that He did not have after his baptism. Deprived of the usual conditions of life, He came upon the essentials of His life -- those inner movements that defined exactly who He was at that time.

This is clearly the case for many inmates at Folsom. With the drudgery and routine, the near total inability to determine your physical conditions, what remains is the choice to evaluate your life at a different, more spiritual, level. The choice to live in the usual way, or to live in a fashion that is consistent with deeper realities of life.

For Jesus, He came to see the outline and contours of His destiny. As one called by His Father to bring all men and women back to the Father on a deep and permanent level. A level that was threatening to the religious powers of His day, but one that is literally eternal for those that choose to follow Him.

Prison can be such a place of initiation, as the desert was for Jesus. It can happen, if one steps outside the usual way of thinking about his life. This is what Jesus meant by "repent". It is not simply about the confession of sin, but more importantly about a radically new way of viewing our life. A contemplative life-style invites this new way of seeing our life by stepping outside the usual way we consider our life.

# The Roofers

Mark 2: 1-12

When He had come back to Capernaum several days afterward, it was heard that He was at home. [2] And many were gathered together, so that there was no longer room, not even near the door; and He was speaking the word to them. [3] And they came, bringing to Him a paralytic, carried by four men. [4] Being unable to get to Him because of the crowd, they removed the roof above Him; and when they had dug an opening, they let down the pallet on which the paralytic was lying. [5] And Jesus seeing their faith said to the paralytic, "Son, your sins are forgiven." [6] But some of the scribes were sitting there and reasoning in their hearts, [7] "Why does this man speak that way? He is blaspheming; who can forgive sins ]but God alone?"

[8] Immediately Jesus, aware in His spirit that they were reasoning that way within themselves, said to them, "Why are you reasoning about these things in your hearts? [9] Which is easier, to say to the paralytic, 'Your sins are forgiven'; or to say, 'Get up, and pick up your pallet and walk?' [10] But so that you may know that the Son of Man has authority on earth to forgive sins"—He said to the paralytic, [11] "I say to you, get up, pick up your pallet and go home." [12] And he got up and immediately picked up the pallet and went out in the sight of everyone, so that they were all amazed and were glorifying God, saying, "We have never seen anything like this."

The men in the Gospel today clearly had strong feelings about their friend who was paralyzed. They knew the whole town was literally at Jesus' doorstep, so they found a creative way to get around the crowd and put their friend right in front of Jesus. They literally broke into the house through the roof in the hope of placing him in front of Jesus. Little did they know how profound this encounter with Jesus would be. Notice it is their love for their friend and their trust in Jesus that heals their friend. The text tells us that it is their faith that prompts Jesus to forgive his sin and remove his shame.

Details of the story say they were "unable to get near Jesus because of the crowd," so they break through the roof. Why are these fine points important?

"Breaking away from the crowd" and finding a unique approach to the Lord seem to go together. It goes on all the time here in prison. It's not obvious and spectacular like the Gospel story, but it is true and profound nonetheless. Someone is alone and suffering in their personal guilt, shame, and grief. Usually they can't sleep. Sometimes the depth of their suffering is such that they can't eat or reach out to anyone. They are alone in their misery. The usual answers provided by "the crowd" the person hangs with -- the hatred, resentment, and violence that controls the crowd-- no longer soothes the depth of their pain.

Then someone, maybe their "cellie," or some other observant individual, not part of the usual crowd, simply reaches out and points to a path through their nightmare. This is the Way of the all-compassionate, forgiving Christ, described in today's reading. They know what the man is going through because they have been there themselves. They know also what Christ can do for him, because He has done it for them. They simply place him before Christ and He takes it from there.

# Why Do We Suffer?

> Mark 1:40-45
> [40] And a leper came to Jesus, beseeching Him and falling on his knees before Him, and saying, "If You are willing, You can make me clean." [41] Moved with compassion, Jesus stretched out His hand and touched him, and said to him, "I am willing; be cleansed." [42] Immediately the leprosy left him and he was cleansed. [43] And He sternly warned him and immediately sent him away, [44] and He said to him, "See that you say nothing to anyone; but go, show yourself to the priest and offer for your cleansing what Moses commanded, as a testimony to them." [45] But he went out and began to proclaim it freely and to spread the news around, to such an extent that Jesus could no longer publicly enter a city, but stayed out in unpopulated areas; and they were coming to Him from everywhere.

People have understandable reactions to their personal sufferings and the sufferings that are so obvious in our world. Our sense of justice and fundamental fairness yearns for an explanation. If our God is as powerful and compassionate as we understand Him to be, how can so much suffering happen in our world?

In the Book of Job, we find Job, a good and decent man, struck down by intolerable and apparently meaningless suffering. His friends tried to convince him this suffering was the result of his somehow angering his God and that God was therefore paying him back in kind. Job didn't buy this explanation. He knew he was a good man. At the end of the Book of Job, God does explain himself to Job with a perspective that satisfies Job, but God does not answer his question. Job came to see that God's ways are not Job's ways.

Job had new-found respect for his God, but no further answer about the "why" of suffering.

A similar dynamic takes place in the Gospel reading from Mark. Here Jesus is literally healing the suffering and broken lives of people who come before him. You'd think this would be the best way to show Jesus' relationship to God Himself. His disciples think they have caught on to Jesus' power and compassion. They find, however, that Jesus will have none of it, and tells them He wants to move on to the next town, as if somehow His healing power was not the answer that would be most helpful to the people encountering him. Sound familiar?

If we do not get the answer to the question of why there is suffering, maybe we are asking the wrong question. Maybe it is not "Why am I suffering?" and not "Why does God permit suffering in the world?" But, how can I change the way I think about suffering in my life and in the world? Perhaps we need to reflect with Job that "God's ways are not my ways." Or, reflect on Jesus' action that suggest that there is something more to suffering than healing it. Perhaps, there is something to the notion that, in today's language, as the poet says: "God writes straight with crooked lines."

# An Invitation from Christ

> ## Mark 1: 14-20
>
> [14] Now after John had been taken into custody, Jesus came into Galilee, preaching the gospel of God, [15] and saying, "The time is fulfilled, and the kingdom of God is at hand; repent and believe in the gospel."
>
> [16] As He was going along by the Sea of Galilee, He saw Simon and Andrew, the brother of Simon, casting a net in the sea; for they were fishermen. [17] And Jesus said to them, "Follow Me, and I will make you become fishers of men." [18] Immediately they left their nets and followed Him. [19] Going on a little farther, He saw James the son of Zebedee, and John his brother, who were also in the boat mending the nets. [20] Immediately He called them; and they left their father Zebedee in the boat with the hired servants, and went away to follow Him.

Mark's account of the beginning of Jesus' ministry takes off like a rocket with Jesus taking over for the arrested John the Baptist, calling four new disciples, and their immediate decision to leave all and follow him. Somehow this narrative seems to move too fast. We need more information on these all-important first encounters with Jesus, whom sometime later, not now, Peter would call "Christ."

Who could this person be in the flesh in order for Peter and the rest of them to literally drop their fishing nets, and leave everything behind to follow him? This, of course, is of critical importance for us, because we must deal with our own encounter with Christ, perhaps in a different form, but an encounter nonetheless. What was it about this person who created this immediate reaction.

The Gospels narrate several encounters of individuals with Christ. People followed him, asking Him for all sorts of favors and healings. For many they just wanted to hear him speak and hang around him. They apparently had no problem approaching him, questioning him, some after his arrest even hitting him in the face and belittling him. He hung out with the bottom rung of society, those who had little or no status or power. The kind of people who were called "unclean" in those days. In our day, we'd call them the "dregs of society." Yet he had no problem at all confronting the powerful and the religious leaders of his time.

What would you expect to find if you were introduced to him, or he came walking by you doing your work at the prison? If he "saw" (verses 16, 19) you, he'd be directly interested in you, you'd have a sense that he knew the deepest, most hidden part of you. No doubt you'd have a sense that he was not judging you for your mistakes, and dumb moves, and at the same time not hesitating to suggest a better way of thinking about life. You'd probably want to continue the conversation. Notice, Jesus would probably not tell you to love him. He wasn't about that.

Do you think you could meet Him? That is, actually meet Him directly? Would you want to? Our Tradition tells us we can meet Him in several ways.

We meet Him in the Gospels, those stories of people who had encounters with Him. Reading these stories gives us a feel for who He is, since we know that the Risen Jesus, Christ Our Lord, in some mysterious way, is the same human person people met those many years ago. We meet Him by becoming aware that His Spirit can live inside of us by our awareness of our yearning for an encounter with Him.

> ### John 1: 35-42
>
> [35] Again the next day John was standing with two of his disciples, [36] and he looked at Jesus as He walked, and said, "Behold, the Lamb of God!" [37] The two disciples heard him speak, and they followed Jesus. [38] And Jesus turned and saw them following, and said to them, "What do you seek?" They said to Him, "Rabbi (which translated means Teacher), where are You staying?" [39] He said to them, "Come, and you will see." So they came and saw where He was staying; and they stayed with Him that day, for it was about the tenth hour. [40] One of the two who heard John speak and followed Him, was Andrew, Simon Peter's brother. [41] He found first his own brother Simon and said to him, "We have found the Messiah" (which translated means Christ). [42] He brought him to Jesus. Jesus looked at him and said, "You are Simon the son of John; you shall be called Cephas" (which is translated Peter).

Today's Gospel is the beginning of the narrative of the life, death and resurrection of Jesus according to John. The story is deceptively simple. John the Baptist is standing with two of his disciples, waiting and watching. Jesus makes His entrance onto the stage by walking along. John announces the arrival of "The Lamb," and the two disciples follow Jesus, at least to a distance wherein Jesus might notice that He is being followed. The question Jesus asks them, Jesus will ask others in various ways during the rest of the Gospel. "What do you want?" Like most of us, the disciples seem intimidated by this apparently simple question. They respond by asking "Teacher, where do you live?"

If we lived in the first century, and understood Greek, the disciples' simple question to Jesus would trigger all sorts of meanings because they were not asking Jesus about his residence. They were really asking: What is the meaning of your life? What is your life's purpose? Suddenly, this question becomes a plea for help in knowing where we struggling human beings can find the peace and happiness we seek. Isn't this the most important question in our own life? If we were there with the disciples, we'd ask Jesus the same question.

Jesus' short answer gives the key to discovering the meaning and purpose of our life. He tells them "Come and see." Jesus invites them to more than they are expecting. "You will find where I am staying in more ways than one." In today's language Jesus is saying "Come and hang out with me and you'll find your meaning and purpose in life."

Notice Jesus is not giving a mental concept, or some intellectual explanation of God's demands for us. Rather he invites them and us to come to him and to walk with him and to learn from him, for only in this way will we discover the truth about God's love for us, and about our need to join Jesus in loving others. Nothing we can learn is more important than this.

I believe there is a moment for each of us when we come to realize that there must be more to life than we were led to believe. That there must be a meaning in life that is more than street smarts and worldly wisdom can offer. We see that our life is truly "unmanageable" because we can't find the way to lasting peace and happiness by our schemes for success, power, and dominance.

From this deeply meaningful gospel episode, we learn two significant principles. First, the most important precondition for conversion to a new way of living is recognizing the profound inner yearning we have for wholeness and completion in our life. And, second, the path toward wholeness and peace is the path of Jesus' invitation. Come and see selfless love in all His encounters and Selfless Love will come to us, and in this encounter we will find the wholeness and peace of our heart's desire.

> *"The only true joy on earth is to escape from the prison of our own false self and enter by love into union with the Life that dwells and sings in the essence of every creature and in the core of our own soul."*
> Thomas Merton, *New Seeds of Contemplation*

# The One Important Truth

> ## John 3:16-18
> [16] "For God so loved the world, that He gave His only begotten Son, that whoever believes in Him shall not perish, but have eternal life. [17] For God did not send the Son into the world to judge the world, but that the world might be saved through Him. [18] He who believes in Him is not judged; he who does not believe has been judged already, because he has not believed in the name of the only begotten Son of God.

Several people who come to chapel, "lifers" who have been in prison for many years, have a special wisdom, gained through experience of living life here at Folsom Prison. This wisdom is not written in a book. It is a lived wisdom of the gut, a wisdom born of first-hand experience gained the hard way -- through painful day-in day-out living.

The core of the wisdom comes from the credibility of the "lifer" himself. By his very life, one can tell that he lives the wisdom he is teaching. His words have power because his way of life works for him. So we call this wisdom "the truth." It is the one important piece of information that allows him to live in prison as a free man.

In the same way, the Gospel today focuses on the One Truth, the Only Important Truth, that Jesus is trying to teach his followers. It is the basic teaching of Jesus, repeated over and over again, in different ways, in different forms, in Jesus' words and in his actions. The One Important Truth is this:

*Jesus is God's Son*
*He has come into the world bringing God's own life*
*So that every person who believes Him also has God's own life*
*And is now permanently accepted into God's inner life.*

What then does it mean to "believe" Jesus? What does it mean to "believe" the lifer who has transformed his life? It is not having "faith" as we usually hear it. It is closer to trust. With the lifer, just hanging around him creates the trust. The same is true of Jesus - just hanging around him, watching him, listening to him creates the trust necessary to "believe" in him.

We tend to believe the transformed lifer because we recognize we don't know what we are doing. We don't know what truth about ourselves to believe. We end up believing in Jesus for many of the same reasons. Though we have no idea of the inner life of God, Jesus has the credibility to teach us. We can take the step to trust him. He'll take us the rest of the way.

> ### Matthew 16:21-23
> [21] From that time Jesus began to show His disciples that He must go to Jerusalem, and suffer many things from the elders and chief priests and scribes, and be killed, and be raised up on the third day. [22] Peter took Him aside and began to rebuke Him, saying, "God forbid it, Lord! This shall never happen to You." [23] But He turned and said to Peter, "Get behind Me, Satan! You are a stumbling block to Me; for you are not setting your mind on God's interests, but man's."

Three times in the gospel of Matthew Jesus has a dramatic confrontation with Peter. Each has its own specific meaning, and today's intense argument cuts into the deep notions of who Peter is and what this "Church" that Jesus says Peter will lead is all about.

There is no doubt that Jesus and Peter engaged, even triggered, each other. You may recall Jesus granted Peter's colossal, spontaneous request. Peter did indeed walk on water, just like the Lord Himself, until he let his fear get the better of him. With this, Jesus, seemingly shaken Himself, genuinely asks Peter: "why didn't you trust me?"

In another face to face encounter, Peter responds eloquently to Jesus' question of "Who do you say that I am?" with the famous: "You are the Anointed One, the Son of God." Peter's unashamed declaration is met by Jesus' own declaration of Peter being the foundation of Jesus' "church." This moment of triumphant mutual declaration is enshrined in Catholic Christian holy places throughout the world. Far fewer holy places throughout the world enshrine the words of today's gospel.

In today's gospel, we hear that this "Anointed One" must soon suffer terribly, be humiliated and mocked by his own clan, tortured and executed. And perhaps worse, the one whom Jesus thought knew Him so well, the one Jesus relies on to lead Jesus' followers, he himself simply cannot, and will not, accept this outcome! So Jesus tells him off.

What did Peter not understand that led to this condemnation? Tradition answers: the Messiah was not to be leader of a human kingdom, but a divine kingdom established by the Father. But how did Peter miss this fundamental point when getting it so right only moments before?

Perhaps Peter was the first to make the mistakes we all make, the mistake that the Church, like its first leader, has made down through the centuries: we continue to interpret the life of Christ from the perspective of the educated, clergy class, rather than from the perspective of the marginalized, poor and the oppressed. In the gospels, it's the lame, the blind, the prostitutes, the drunkards, the tax collectors, the sinners, the outsiders, the foreigners who tend to follow Jesus.

When Jesus spoke about Peter leading his "Church" he was not referring to the hierarchical institution we frequently invoke for this saying. After all, the hierarchical institution of Jesus' own religion at the time was His fiercest enemy. Jesus meant something different. The root meaning of "Church" is something much deeper, and more personal. It is the group that holds the Mystery together. Losing sight of the Mystery of Christ throwing his lot with the lowest of the low, we lose sight of who Jesus really is, and what his Church is all about.

> ### Matthew 15:21-28
>
> [21] Jesus went away from there, and withdrew into the district of Tyre and Sidon. [22] And a Canaanite woman from that region came out and began to cry out, saying, "Have mercy on me, Lord, Son of David; my daughter is cruelly demon-possessed." [23] But He did not answer her a word. And His disciples came and implored Him, saying, "Send her away, because she keeps shouting at us." [24] But He answered and said, "I was sent only to the lost sheep of the house of Israel." [25] But she came and began to bow down before Him, saying, "Lord, help me!" [26] And He answered and said, "It is not good to take the children's bread and throw it to the dogs." [27] But she said, "Yes, Lord; but even the dogs feed on the crumbs which fall from their masters' table." [28] Then Jesus said to her, "O woman, your faith is great; it shall be done for you as you wish." And her daughter was healed at once.

Matthew wrote this story sometime in the mid 70's A.D. to Jewish Christians with deep and intense boundary problems. As Jews, familiar with their heritage and traditions they were forced to include Gentile converts to Christianity who were "foreigners," aliens and outsiders, considered by many Jews to be "unclean."

It is not hard to understand this mentality because it is so prevalent at Folsom prison. Isn't the root of much of the hatred and violence among prisoners the belief that we belong to a group, or a race, or a religion that is "a cut above" the other group? Don't we see ourselves as the privileged ones who belong, and others as the "foreigners?" If Matthew came to speak at Folsom prison, he would tell us the story of this remarkable Canaanite woman.

In the story Jesus actually calls the woman a "dog!" During Jesus' time, gentiles were frequently referred to as dogs by the Jews. Scavengers who ate whatever they found, dogs were considered unclean, as were those who were not members of the Jewish community. At the time Jesus apparently believed that He was sent only to the Jews. The disciples had a simple solution: "...get rid of her" (v.23).

Matthew tells his listeners that Jesus doesn't work like that. He listens to her and discovers she is a person in her own right, who loves her daughter so much she is willing to humiliate herself (v.25) to the One she believes can make her daughter well again. Would we do any differently if our daughter was deeply ill? Matthew is trying to tell his Jewish readers, and us, that the "foreigner," as it turns out, is not much different than we are. Jesus, Himself, came to this change in attitude as he encountered her. As a result, this "foreigner" (a woman no less) changed the entire direction of His mission!

The question for us becomes: who is the "foreigner" in our life at Folsom? Perhaps we are a "foreigner" to someone else? Perhaps our cherished beliefs and values are seen as inferior to the other's beliefs and values. The on-going group drama at Folsom prison doesn't allow this consideration as we seem so lost in our own self-righteousness and preoccupation with retaliation for even the slightest of perceived disrespect.

Matthew is inviting us to another point of view. He is calling us to model our thoughts and actions on the example of Jesus. In God's saving plan for humanity there is no room for an "us versus them" attitude, no exclusion based on gender or race, not even on religion! When we recognize that we are no different than the "foreigner," we can find the deep kinship and true solidarity we have with each other, especially here at Folsom prison. We are all learners, fellow-travelers, trying to find meaning in our lives, facing the One who brings us together, without exclusion, favoritism, or privilege.

# A Contemplative View of the Lord's Passion

> *Jesus is not changing his Father's mind about us; he is changing our mind about what is real and what is not.*
>
> Richard Rohr, OFM, *Things Hidden,* p.189.

## MARK 14:32-42

[32] And they come to a piece of land called Gethsemane and Jesus says to his disciples "Sit here while I pray." [33] And he takes Peter, James, and John with him and he begins to go into shock and be overcome. [34] And he says to them, "I feel so utterly sad that I could die. Stay here and keep watch." [35] And going on a little further he collapsed onto the ground and he prays that if it were possible, the Hour might pass him by. [36] He was saying, "ABBA, Father, all things are possible for you; take away this cup from me; yet not as I will, but as you will." [37] And he comes and finds [the disciples] sleeping. And he says to Peter, "Simon, are you sleeping? Do you not have the strength to keep watch for a single hour? [38] Keep watch and pray so that you may not enter into temptation. The spirit is eager, but the flesh is week." [39] And going away he prayed, using the same expression. [40] And coming a second time he found them sleeping, for their eyes were very heavy. They did not know how to answer him. [41] And he comes a third time and says to them, "You can sleep from now on and take your rest; it is all over. The Hour has come, and behold, the Human One is betrayed into the hands of the sinners. [42] Rise. Let us go forth. Behold the one who is betraying me approaches."

(Translation by Michael Casey.)

The drama of the Lord's passion, his betrayal, arrest, trial, conviction, tortuous death, and final vindication starts with his encounter with his "Father". This scene has come to be known as the "Agony in the Garden," or "Gethsemane" which is the place just outside of Jerusalem where the encounter took place.

This scene has a particular meaning for men in prison as it holds the key to true inner freedom, if only we have the eyes to see it.

The scene shows a Jesus we are not used to seeing. It shows his inner consciousness like few other scenes. For one thing, in our time, we come to think of Jesus as always possessing a confident reliance on the ultimate mystery that he called "Father." Not so here, at least at first sight.

His going into "shock" and being "overcome" (v. 33) describe a person experiencing a severe trauma. We can only guess at the origins of the trauma. As children we were taught that he had divine knowledge of his impending torture and death. But now, as so many of us face our own inner traumas and experiences of a lifetime, maybe we have a better clue as to his agony. It appears to be a profound disturbance in his soul.

He tells his friends "I feel so utterly sad that I could die." (v. 34) He looks to his friends, as we would, for support. He is not testing them. He does not want to do this alone. This is the deep internal struggle of a leader coming to terms with the consequences of his revolutionary teaching. The Source of his teaching, namely his relationship with his Father, appears not to help him even now in the final hours of his life.

What does he do? Cut and run (he could have), or stand his ground? Who among us in the deep terror of our dark nights have not come upon this same dilemma? Do we face our inner demons, or cut and run to the closest diversion or addiction that will once again distract us from the reality of our inner life?

Now comes the pivotal moment of the scene, this is his answer to his dilemma: "Yet not as I will but as you will" (v. 36). For those familiar with Centering Prayer, this "Yet" is Jesus' Sacred Word. This "Yet not as I will but as you will' is Jesus" consent to the presence and action of the Father in his life. No different than the consent we give when we use our Sacred Word in the depths of our Centering Prayer experience. Jesus is saying, as we are saying, I submit to You, because it is not about me it is about You.

Commentators talk about Jesus "obedience" to the Father here. But this is no ordinary obedience, as in "I'll do what you tell me because you're in charge." No, this obedience comes from a recognition that the Father is deserving of his trust. It is a re-framing of his inner conflict in the light of his relationship with the Father. It comes from Jesus' life-long, intimate relationship with the Father, and it is this intimate relationship we call Contemplation. The heart of the contemplative experience, the 'silence' of contemplative prayer, is the recognition that God is indeed with us. God doesn't tell us in words, but the realization of his presence is just as real.

Out of Jesus' contemplative experience of the Father, his "resting" or "abiding," his true destiny is formed. In the middle of his night terror he remembers the faithfulness of his Father, even though he may not experience His closeness in the middle of his terror. Jesus' "Yet" is the turning point of the entire passion story. It explains the near absolute silence of Jesus in the next 24 hours of the drama.

Now, even before his arrest, he can say to his overwhelmed companions "it is all over." He has found his way, he can get up off the ground and support his friends to do the same (v. 42). If we can bear the internal torment, we, too, come to find our destiny in the still moments of our prayer. Through our freedom we will find our destiny, if we have the eyes to see it.

# The Coming of Christ, Our Brother

## Luke 2: 1-14

Now in those days a decree went out from Caesar Augustus, that a census be taken of all the inhabited earth. [2] This was the first census taken while Quirinius was governor of Syria. [3] And everyone was on his way to register for the census, each to his own city. [4] Joseph also went up from Galilee, from the city of Nazareth, to Judea, to the city of David which is called Bethlehem, because he was of the house and family of David, [5] in order to register along with Mary, who was engaged to him, and was with child. [6] While they were there, the days were completed for her to give birth. [7] And she gave birth to her firstborn son; and she wrapped Him in cloths, and laid Him in a manger, because there was no room for them in the inn.

[8] In the same region there were some shepherds staying out in the fields and keeping watch over their flock by night. [9] And an angel of the Lord suddenly stood before them, and the glory of the Lord shone around them; and they were terribly frightened. [10] But the angel said to them, "Do not be afraid; for behold, I bring you good news of great joy which will be for all the people; [11] for today in the city of David there has been born for you a Savior, who is Christ the Lord. [12] This will be a sign for you: you will find a baby wrapped in cloths and lying in a manger." [13] And suddenly there appeared with the angel a multitude of the heavenly host praising God and saying, [14] "Glory to God in the highest, And on earth peace among men with whom He is pleased."

By now we are very familiar with the Christmas story: Mary and Joseph leave Nazareth, travel to Bethlehem, and have their child. Angels tell shepherds who themselves witness to this child born in a stable, laid in a feeding basket because there was no room for them in the inn. In fact, we are so familiar with the story that as we hear it, our minds are distracted and we drift off to the joy and sadness of past Christmases and time spent alone during the holidays. We get caught up in these memories, moving quickly away from the reality of the birth of Christ to the culture of the Christmas season. When we make this shift, we miss the dramatic reality of the Divine coming into our world, and an opportunity to accept the invitation of Christmas.

We are told simply that this child, Jesus, born of the poor, young Jewish girl is the Son of God, Christ the Savior, the Liberator of his people and Liberator of us. Yet it took the Church well over 300 years to even begin to describe in words what this reality actually means. Their formula is simply this: at his birth Jesus was "fully human and fully divine."

If he was "fully human" then, like the rest of us, he had to learn about how to live in his world, and discover who he was. Like us, if he was "fully human," he had to learn about friendship, and make mistakes about his own identity. He had to learn to trust his parents, believe his rabbi, and follow his call to personal integrity. Just as we do. Most importantly for us, he had to learn about God and cope with the Divine inviting him into a deep and intimate relationship. Just as we do.

But if he was also at the same time "fully divine," as our Tradition tells us, then his human maturing process was made all the more complicated. This is where the Christmas story takes on personal meaning for each of us. Jesus had to come to terms with the Divine breaking into his life in powerful ways. It makes no sense to think that the reality of the Divine in his life was easy or natural, or without conflict -- for this would not be "human." Like us, he must have been confused, fearful, and at times angry, at the utter mysterious notion of the powerful way the Divine was impacting the outcome of his life. Remember this "fully human, fully divine" person did not become "King of the World." Rather he was rejected by his religious authorities, arrested, put on trial, convicted and executed.

If he was "like us in all things," as St. Paul says, then he was touched and taken by the suffering around him. And, judging from things he said as an adult, he was deeply annoyed at the way the religious leaders of his time laid heavy guilt burdens on people who had sincere spiritual inclinations. And yet, because he was "fully divine" he could respond to people in the way we believe only the Divine can do. If one looks closely at Jesus' life it becomes clear that it was his trust in his relationship with God that explains so much of his identity. It was the human faith of Jesus that becomes the single most important factor in his life.

Recognizing the faith of Jesus in the Divine (for whom he used the most intimate word "Father"), we arrive at the heart of the mystery of Christmas. Christmas is actually celebrating the intimate joining of the Divine and the human in the person of Jesus, the Christ. God Himself in the Person of Christ has become our brother. As our brother, our modest, little human life is forever intimately joined into the Divine Life Itself. Merry Christmas!

> *"You are as You are, and*
> *I am as I am. That which I am*
> *I offer you, Lord God,*
> *For you are it entirely."*

The Cloud of Unknowing

# Suggestions for Further Reading

Bourgeault, Cynthia. Centering Prayer and Inner Awakening.
Cambridge, Massachusetts: Cowley Publications. 2004

Finley, James. Merton's Palace of Nowhere: 25th Anniversary Edition..
Notre Dame, Indiana: Ave Maria Press. 2003.

Keating, Thomas. Open Mind, Open Heart: 20th Anniversary Edition.
New York: Continuum. 2006.

_____. Intimacy With God. New York: Crossroads Publishing. 2000.

_____. Invitation To Love: The Way of Christian Contemplation.
New York: Continuum. 2004.

_____. The Human Condition. New York: Paulist Press. 1999.

May, Gerald. Addiction and Grace. San Francisco:
Doubleday and Company. 1975.

Mayers, Gregory. Listen to the Desert: Secrets of Spiritual Maturity from
the Desert Fathers and Mothers. Missouri: Triumph Books. 1996.

Merton, Thomas. Contemplative Prayer. New York: Image Books. 1996.

Rohr, Richard. Everything Belongs: The Gift of Contemplative Prayer.
New York: Crossroads Publishing. 2003.

## Further Resources

Contemplative Outreach:
10 Park Place, Second Floor Suite B., Butler, NJ 07405
contemplativeoutreach.org.

Center for Action and Contemplation,
PO Box 12464, Albuquerque, NM 87195-2464
(505)242-9588 cac.org

## ABOUT THE AUTHOR

Ray Leonardini is a former lawyer who practiced government and nonprofit law for nearly thirty years. After his retirement he turned toward his foremost area of interest: the Christian spiritual journey. For the last five years, as a Volunteer Chaplain, he has led meditation groups and taught Contemplative Prayer and the Spiritual Journey at Folsom State Prison in California. He is also the Director of the Prison Contemplative Fellowship an association of current and former prison inmates committed to reaching out to prisoners and their families on their travels along the spiritual path.

Some members of the Prison Contemplative Fellowship

13144106R00063

Made in the USA
San Bernardino, CA
10 July 2014